Photography: pp. 14, 21 (bottom), 25, 29 (top), 135, 161 by the author; pp. 16, 21 (top), 24 (bottom), 32, 36, 54, 78 by Daren Decoteau; title page and pp. 12, 17, 24 (top), 74, 100, 105, 109, 136, 141, 148 (top), 164, 165, 173, 176, 181, 184, 185, 196, 201, 204, 205 (top), 212, 213, 216, 220, 224, by C. Bickford; pp. 92, 101 (bottom), 108, 149, 200 (bottom) by Dr. J. Moore; pp. 57 (top), 152 (bottom), 156 (bottom), 157 by L. Rubin; pp. 33, 37, 156 (top), 180, 189, 192, 193, 197 by G. Lilienthal; pp. 73, 101 (top), 132 (bottom), 148 (bottom), 152 (top), 153 (bottom), 160, 169 (bottom), 221 by Dr. I. Huff; p. 80 by H. Schultz; p. 45 by V. Serex; pp. 144-45 by T. Brosset; pp. 31, 46, 49, 199, 202, 239 by H. Lacey; p. 63 by L. Arnall; pp. 22, 23, 26, 29 (bottom), 44, 56, 171, 182, 219, 222 by L. Van der Meid; pp. 18, 20, 30 (top), 34, 38, 39, 40, 43, 55, 65, 66, 70, 97, 133, 168, 177, 205 (bottom) by Dr. H. Axelrod; p. 140 by P. Leysen; p. 135 by E. Grossman; pp. 83, 104, 112, 113, 116, 117, 120, 121, 124, 125, 128, 129, 132 (top), 153 (top), 169 (top), 172, 188, 200 (top), 207, 217 courtesy of Vogelpark Walsrode; p. 107 courtesy of the New York Zoological Society; p. 137 (top) by Jacobson of Denmark. *Certain other photos credited individually.*

ENDPAPERS Courtesy of Vogelpark Walsrode.

ISBN 0-87666-892-9

t.f.h.

© Copyright 1983 by TFH Publications, Inc. Ltd.

Distributed in the UNITED STATES by T.F.H. Publications, Inc., 211 West Sylvania Avenue, Neptune City, NJ 07753; in CANADA by H & L Pet Supplies Inc., 27 Kingston Crescent, Kitchener, Ontario N2B 2T6; Rolf C. Hagen Ltd., 3225 Sartelon Street, Montreal 382 Quebec; in ENGLAND by T.F.H. (Great Britain) Ltd., 11 Ormside Way, Holmethorpe Industrial Estate, Redhill, Surrey RH1 2PX; in AUSTRALIA AND THE SOUTH PACIFIC by T.F.H. (Australia) Pty. Ltd., Box 149, Brookvale 2100 N.S.W., Australia; in NEW ZEALAND by Ross Haines & Son, Ltd., 18 Monmouth Street, Grey Lynn, Auckland 2 New Zealand; in SINGAPORE AND MALAYSIA by MPH Distributors Pte., 71-77 Stamford Road, Singapore 0617; in the PHILIPPINES by Bio-Research, 5 Lippay Street, San Lorenzo Village, Makati, Rizal; in SOUTH AFRICA by Multipet Pty. Ltd., 30 Turners Avenue, Durban 4001. Published by T.F.H. Publications Inc., Ltd., the British Crown Colony of Hong Kong.

The Handbook of
Amazon Parrots

DR. A.E. DECOTEAU

Dedication

This book is dedicated to Helen I. Decoteau, my wife, for her great support and assistance. Without her help it could not have been completed.

Acknowledgments

I wish to thank Cliff Bickford for his excellent photos of Amazon parrots. Cliff has been a dedicated supporter of the Amazon. The author also wishes to thank Dr. Irwin Huff for his photos of Amazons. Dr. Huff continues to be an able student of the Amazon.

We also wish to thank Dr. W. T. Greene, author of the book *Parrots In Captivity*. In my opinion, Dr. Greene was the finest writer of nineteenth century bird books involving parrots. His *Parrots in Captivity* is highly desirable even to-day.

We also wish to thank Gary and Janet Lilienthal, Dr. John Moore and Linda Rubin for their assistance and photos of Amazons. Finally, I wish to thank Daren, Jay and Kevin Decoteau for their able assistance in my studies of living Amazon parrots.

Contents

> Vitamin Deficiency ... Aspergillosis ...
> Bumblefoot ... Bronchitis ... Cataracts ...
> Chills ... Convulsion ... Conjunctivitis ...
> Constipation ... Crop Binding ... Crop
> Sickness ... Egg Binding ... Enteritis ... Im-
> pacted Gizzard ... Indigestion ... Overgrown
> Beak ... Overgrown Claws ... Pneumonia ...
> Scabies .. Internal Parasites

About the Author

Dr. A. E. Decoteau is a veterinarian with much experience in aviculture as well as the zoo world. He has practiced in zoo veterinary medicine and medicine in aviculture.

He is a judge of parrots and finches and has judged numerous shows throughout the world. He is active as the President of the New Hampshire Cagebird Association and is a member of the American Federation of Aviculture, the African Lovebird Society, the American Cockatiel Society and the Aviculture Society of America.

As an exhibitor, he has won some top awards including Best Amazon over a large entry, Best In Show on three occasions and Second Best In Show on two occasions.

Dr. Decoteau's achievements in the field of aviculture are highlighted by his breeding results. He has successfully bred and raised six hatches of scarlet macaws and six hatches of cockatoos, which included Moluccan, umbrella and lesser sulfur-crested cockatoos. He successfully bred seven different types of Amazons including a recent hatch of the Panama Amazon.

Dr. Decoteau has authored numerous articles for various avicultural magazines and zoological bulletins. His articles have appeared in *Cage-Bird Magazine* and *Agapornis World,* among others.

Dr. Decoteau is currently involved as a director of the New England Conference of Bird Associations.

Preface

During the 1960's there was a tremendous increase in the public's interest in parrots, especially Amazon parrots. Prior to this period all parrot-type birds had been banned for a number of years from coming into the United States, the ban resulting from a fear of the disease psittacosis. With the advent of antibiotics, the danger was greatly decreased. Consequently parrots, including Amazons, started coming into the country in relatively great numbers. By the early 1970's a constant increase in the number of birds imported had occurred until a fear of another bird disease, Newcastle disease, caused a ban by the Department of Agriculture. Within two years of the institution of the ban, the advent of commercial quarantine stations allowed the importation of thousands of additional birds, many of them being Amazons. By 1979 the bird business had experienced a tenfold increase; the number of quarantine stations, for example, grew from twelve to ninety-two.

The popularity of Amazon parrots has kept pace with the growth in popularity of other parrots. In many ways it has even surpassed it, because the Amazons are among the best of all parrot pets.

Distinguished by their intelligence and their talking ability, Amazons make interesting and entertaining pets. Pictured here is a green-cheeked Amazon, *Amazona viridigenalis*.

Chapter 1
The Amazon Parrots

Ranging far from the long, active, wandering Amazon river are a number of diversified parrots named after this magnificent river of South America. These parrots extend from Mexico in southern North America to literally every country of Central and South America as well as the islands of the Caribbean.

All Amazons have short squared-off tails averaging four inches in length. Many of them display their tails by fanning them out, creating a beautiful sight. Amazons also utilize their ability to raise their nape feathers, thereby achieving a fierce display. Perhaps the most remarkable display put on by an Amazon parrot by raising the nape feathers and fanning the tail is that of the hawkheaded parrot. I feel that the hawkheaded parrot is truly a colorful bird, and we shall treat it as an Amazon, even though taxonomists place it in the genus *Deroptyus,* not *Amazona.* Undoubtedly there will be much debate concerning such a move, but such debate can be very healthy and is therefore welcome.

Most Amazons are more or less green in color. They are differentiated from each other primarily by the markings of the head and face. Many, in fact, derive their scientific names from their color and morphology. A few are differentiated by their size only. Most dark green Amazons have green feathers edged in black; this is a common trait of the Amazon. Two or three species, however, are very different in coloration from the other Amazons; they are very colorful.

In general, the Amazon parrots can be divided into five major groups:

- Sixteen species have red dappling on the wings.
- Eight species have blue wing coverts.
- Thirteen species have edges of wings and wing coverts marked with red.
- Fourteen species have red on the head.
- Twelve species have yellow on the head.

Keep in mind that some species overlap in that they show more than one characteristic of the group of five listed. The characteristics are not mutually exclusive.

Most Amazon parrots have an over-all green basic coloring to body and wings, with major distinctions in coloration lying mainly in different colors and markings about the area of the head. Shown is *Amazona ventralis.* Photo by Dr. Herbert R. Axelrod.

Historically, Amazon parrots have been known since before the time of Linnaeus. The first Amazon known to the European world was the Cuban Amazon, discovered on the island of Cuba by a man named Aldrovandi and later named by Linnaeus. Aldrovandi was known to say that the Cuban Amazon was extremely talkative and loved to imitate dogs and cats. The Cuban Amazon was extremely gregarious and quite destructive to fruit trees. Consequently, the Cubans made many parrot pies. In England, the Cuban Amazon was exhibited at shows as early as 1883. Today if a judge were presented with a Cuban Amazon to judge, he would probably pass out with shock. That is how rare they are today in the United States.

It has been said that the African grey is the best talking parrot. Many will disagree and state that the Amazons are better talkers. At any rate, we can state that the Amazons are excellent talkers.

It makes one wonder in amazement when an old Amazon parrot never says "I love bread and butter" until the family sits down to dinner. Sam, our plain-colored Amazon, never says "Answer the phone" until it rings. Our Panama never says "I love you" except to the children of the family. And when angry one of our Amazons says "Naughty Naughty" or "Don't bite hard." This all makes one wonder about the comprehension power of a parrot. We do know that parrots in general and the Amazons in particular are among the most intelligent birds.

It is also noted that males generally are better talkers than females. Amazons will not hesitate to talk in front of strangers. Sometimes they say absolutely nothing. In contrast, noisy Amazons will screech, talk, mimic and whistle while spreading their tails and wings and contracting the pupils of their eyes, all at the same time. In general, the large Amazon parrots are good talkers and the small species are poor talkers.

Other antics of the Amazon are often humorous. Frequently I receive mail from owners of Amazons concerning these antics. One lady wanted to get rid of her yellow-naped Amazon because of the disgusting habit of its throwing up its food, always in her hand. If she didn't touch the Amazon the bird would "throw up" in the cage. I informed her that regurgitation is the greatest proof of affection one can receive from an Amazon. The bird is merely trying to regurgitate to the owner just as it may do to a mate or a baby Amazon.

Perhaps the antic which hurts the Amazon parrots' popularity the most is their loud screeching, often produced at inappropriate times. This turns some people off, and occasionally people will sell their noisy birds. However, we can vouch that the good attributes of Amazon parrots far outweigh the bad.

Sam, the author's plain-colored Amazon, eagerly accepts an ice cream cone.

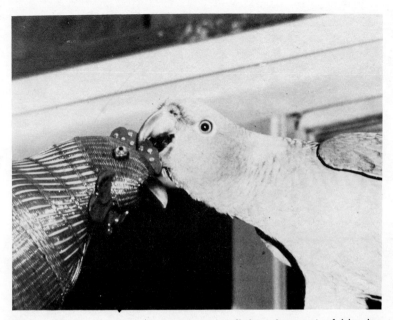

This rugged old rooster is having the fight taken out of him by Charlie, a yellow-naped Amazon owned by Mr. and Mrs. Oscar R. Willingham.

Perhaps the most notable of parrot aviculturists and authors was W.T. Greene, active in the late 1880's. Greene compared an ape to an Amazon parrot this way:

"The ape from his external form, so like the human, his gestures and gait; the rude resemblance of his face to that of man, from the analogous arrangement of all his organs with ours, has been regarded as a species of imperfect and wild man.

"Had he received the gift of speech, like the parrot, he would have passed for a genuine man in the eyes of the multitude. The parrot is in the orders of bird what the ape is in that of viviparous quadrupeds. It would appear that the parrot is still more closely connected with us than the latter because the communion of speech is more intimate than that of mere sign and gesture .."

Pet shops offer a good variety of different types of cages suitable for Amazon parrots, and in general a good rule to follow is to use the largest parrot-type cage available—but keeping Amazons (such as the white-fronted Amazon, *Amazona albifrons,* shown here) in spacious aviaries offers a number of advantages. Photo by Dr. M. Vriends.

Chapter 2
Housing Amazon Parrots

Housing is most important for both pet Amazons and breeding Amazons. If you have a pet Amazon, it is worthwhile to look for a very large cage suitable for a macaw or a large monkey. Use nothing smaller. You will find that your Amazon will be happier. As you work with your bird it will be opportune to take him out of the cage at certain periods of the day. At any rate, your Amazon should be able to flap his wings freely with much room to spare. Surprisingly, breeding pairs of Amazons have nested in similar caging; however, we believe that an aviary at least 6 x 6 x 6 feet is more conducive to the breeding habits of the birds of the genus *Amazona*.

We have utilized a walk-in aviary 8 feet long by 6 feet wide by 8 feet high. This aviary is supplied with two or three hollow logs for nesting. These logs are placed at medium height to high in the pen. We place feeding stands just inside the door (with special opening areas, since breeding Amazons can become dangerously pugnacious). These feeding and watering pans are placed at a medium height within the aviary. In another instance we utilized a pen 7 feet high, 4 feet wide and 10 feet long. Using this setup with hollow logs and a similar feeding arrangement to the former setup, we were pleased at the acceptance by the Amazons.

However, our constant study of most Amazons has revealed that they exercise very little by flying within the aviary; they prefer climbing around, using their feet and strong beak. They screech and chatter a lot but don't fly very much.

Therefore we tried a new aviary for a pair of Panama Amazons. Into an aviary four feet square we placed a square nest box about the size of a cockatiel nest box, only with a larger entrance hole, in the hope that the Panamas would apply themselves to this unit. The nest box measured 12x12x18 inches. The pair of Amazons immediately took to the aviary and the nest box. Within two weeks the female had laid three eggs and started incubating. We eventually had one chick hatch with success and raised him to adulthood. During the incubation period the male spent most of his time on the perch outside the nest box.

Nest boxes the size of these used for cockatiels can be attractive to Amazon breeding pairs.

Amazons like this young Tres Marias need aviaries made from strong wire on which they can climb. *Below:* for Amazons nesting in aviaries, this hollow log would be ideal.

21

Whether the perch provided for an Amazon parrot is of the manufactured type purchased in pet shops or of unshaped and untreated natural tree branches, the perch will be worked over by the parrot's beak. The Finsch's Amazon shown here hasn't yet had a chance to work over the branch on which it perches. Photo by Dr. M. Vriends.

In another aviary of 10x4x7 feet, our pair of Santo Domingo Amazons decided to nest in a hollow log. This pair would fly from log to feeding pans more frequently than most other Amazons would fly. They too were successful in laying eggs. They laid two and hatched them both, raising the babies to maturity.

We prefer a black dirt base in most of our aviaries, as the Amazons not only get much good out of the minerals in the dirt but also can fluff their feathers in this dirt by using it as a dry bath. Our attempt at placing vegetation into the Amazon aviaries was unsuccessful. Amazons tend to completely denude all vegetation. They also chew the wood to bits. Consequently, the chain link fence is the best type of

A cage intended for housing an Amazon parrot should provide as a minimum space requirement enough room for the bird to flap its wings comfortably, with no danger of banging the wings into the bars of the cage. Photo by Dr. Herbert R. Axelrod.

This cage is too small to be used for anything other than transporting this Cuban Amazon.

An ideal litter base for parrot aviaries is ground corncob which remains dry—this Grand Cayman Amazon loves it.

These baby Santa Domingo Amazons are being held by the author's sons while on a visit to the Dominican Republic.

material one can use in building housing for these parrots. I have also used hardware cloth with no problems. For some reason they don't bother this material.

It is advisable to place branches within the aviary for the birds' use in chewing to prevent boredom. We suggest that you do not use cherry wood, since it can cause poisoning from prussic acid.

In summation, one can successfully breed Amazons in small units as well as large flights. Just don't keep your breeders or your pet Amazon too cramped. The birds want freedom to move about when they desire.

To keep your Amazon healthy and alert you must provide it with a proper diet; this is especially important for breeding Amazons. Pictured here is a blue-crowned Amazon, *Amazona farinosa guatemalae*. Photo by Dr. Herbert R. Axelrod.

Chapter 3
Feeding The Amazons

The subject of feeding is complex when discussing various categories in the bird fancy, but the pet owner can get along well by feeding a standard and routine mixture which can include the usual choice items your Amazons love.

Firstly, the basic love of all Amazon parrots and their first choice is sunflower seeds. Sunflower seeds are rather fattening, and the amount of them fed to your bird should be controlled if you notice your pet Amazon gaining too much weight. You might wish to switch to safflower seeds. Safflower seeds are much less fattening and don't contain fatty acids contained in sunflower seeds. Fruits and vegetables should be a necessity; we suggest you feed the type favored by your bird, as individual birds have different preferences. We have some Amazons that prefer apples, while others prefer bananas, some love oranges and still others are partial to celery.

Don't let anyone tell you that you can't spoil your Amazon with a piece of chocolate now and then. They love it.

When we lived in Puerto Rico, we were visited by a lovely couple in their fifties. They wanted me to see their ancient but colorful and still exciting yellow-naped Amazon. He was 105 years old and had a complete history. Elsewhere we shall expound on his longevity. The gentleman indicated that for years this bird had had two pieces of chocolate candy daily. Through its entire life it was fed many bananas, apples and citrus fruits.

The aviculturist must feed somewhat differently if he intends to breed successfully or if he has many birds to feed daily. Certainly, many of the following diets can readily be used by the single pet owner in addition to the diet already described.

If you want to successfully breed Amazons, you must be knowledgeable about feeding practices. I firmly believe that of all the parrots in the world the Amazons are the most difficult to breed and successfully rear. Through the years, I have been fortunate in hatching and rearing no fewer than seven species of Amazons.

During the pre-breeding conditioning process, sunflower seed must be used sparingly, perhaps only two days per week, or your females will become too fat, with too much fatty tissue in the oviduct area and much less fertility. Likewise, the male can fatten too quickly and lack libido, with a consequent decrease in fertility.

We suggest using five other food mixtures for breeding Amazons. In the first mixture we start by boiling a sufficient supply of rice until well cooked. The amount varies with the number of birds fed. To this rice and rice water are added enough raisins to make up twenty percent of the total. To this is added dry dog food, which should be fifty percent of the total. This thick, somewhat wet and warm mixture is fed immediately. This mixture is fed twice weekly.

The second mixture is a bit more difficult to prepare. We take two pounds of wheat flour, three pounds of corn meal, four pounds of parakeet seed, one cup of a powdered vitamin complex, one cup of baking powder, one cup buttermilk, six cups of eggs (shells included) and one cup of safflower oil. This is mixed thoroughly and baked for forty minutes at 400 degrees F. It is cooled until just warm, then readily fed to all our Amazons. They devour this mixture. Because of the tedious preparation involved, we prepare and feed this mixture only once per week.

Our third mixture consists of a fruit concoction, and its makeup of course depends on the availability of fruits.

Amazons are able to feed themselves by clutching food in their powerful claws. *Below:* this open stand has containers for four different food mixtures; the metal band around the bottom tray is a safeguard against chewing and the formica tray facilitates cleaning.

This closeup of a blue-crowned Amazon reveals the typically power-ful beak of the average Amazon parrot—a piece of equipment that lets Amazons easily open and devour even very hard-shelled items in their normal diet. Photo by Dr. Herbert R. Axelrod.

Once per week we dice up apples, oranges, grapefruits, bananas, pineapples, pears, papayas and cherries. We place the well mixed products in pint packages and freeze. Twice per week we take out our needed supply and thoroughly thaw the mixture before feeding.

Every other week we interchange a vegetable mix for the fruit. This is prepared fresh and fed immediately. We use chopped potatoes (boiled and cold), raw carrots, celery, endive and chicory.

In addition to the four above mixtures, we also prepare a canned dog food mixed with safflower seed. The dog food is mostly meat, a necessity for Amazon parrot parent birds. This is offered in small amounts daily as a supplement. Be-

Though special treats aid in handling and training your bird, they should be given sparingly.

fore we started this high-protein supplement we would have losses in the nest. Many times the parents would kill their own offspring. When babies are in the nest we always offer a bowl of fresh bread and milk to the parents. They devour it, and it assists them in feeding the young. Most of our Amazon babies have been raised by their parents. It is fine to hand-raise baby Amazons if you have the time, but it takes a lot of time. (Details of hand feeding will be presented in a later chapter.) The parents also receive a piece of cheese daily; surprisingly, they look forward to this treat. Every day we add a multi-liquid vitamin to the water. There is one commercial brand that we use constantly.

There are as many feeding plans and avicultural diets as there are aviaries. You may develop your own also. One important point to remember is that certain birds have idiosyncrasies . . . some do not like oranges; others do not like peanuts.

This Grand Cayman Amazon appears to be curious about what two moustache parakeets have to eat.

This double yellow-head Amazon advertises the New Hampshire Cage-bird Association as he nibbles a corner of this booklet.

We use peanuts, preferably raw, as special treats. We believe that special treats will assist in training as well as handling your Amazons. Peanut butter, whole wheat bread, pound cake and marshmallows are used by many breeders, aviculturists and pet owners. We use them only sparingly.

Finally, trainers use sunflower seeds sparingly as a treat instead of as a diet. They are relished so much by the Amazon that they make an excellent tool for training and are withheld from the regular diet for that reason.

If you plan to show your Amazon, it should be tame and easy to handle. Talking to your bird as you handle it will reassure the bird and facilitate taming.

Chapter 4
Amazons In Exhibitions

It is most exciting to exhibit your Amazon in a bird show. Right now in the United States there are numerous shows being staged, with more coming along all the time.

One of the larger parrot shows is the one staged by the New Hampshire Cagebird Association, which holds its show each October in Nashua. The 1978 show proved great for Amazons; 26 birds out of 212 parrots and 418 birds exhibited in total were Amazons. It was even greater for our family as Sam, our faithful and outstanding plain-colored Amazon (*Amazona farinosa inornata*) was selected by judge Harold Yanik as Best Amazon in the show. Sam went on to win second Best South American Parrot. Daren Decoteau's scarlet macaw took Best South American.

Parrots are judged for condition, steadiness, symmetrical balance and comparison to the ideal and those other birds in competition. Condition includes general appearance, quality of feather and general color. Feet and beak are also considered under condition. Steadiness includes the character of the bird.

If the Amazon is flighty or does not stand classy on the perch, he is not steady. *Symmetrical balance* includes the degree of stance on the perch as well as character of the Amazon. The judge should query as to how the particular bird being judged compares to the ideal. Also, how does he compare to other Amazons of his species?

Show committees vary throughout the nation. Some committees group various species, genera, families and even orders of birds together. I believe the ideal classification

Most Amazons are excellent mimics—Sanchita, a Panama Amazon, often cackles like a hen.

Sanchita proudly displays her features as an exhibition bird as she stands next to a trophy.

groups birds by subspecies or species which compete against each other. For example, the yellow-naped Amazons compete against each other. If there are four in the class, the judge will select first, second and third. The first place yellow-naped is then eligible for the competition for Best Amazon. In the 1978 New Hampshire show, the first place winners of the following classes competed for Best Amazon: double yellow head, yellow-naped, Panama, yellow-front, green-cheeked, white-fronted, Santo Domingo, yellow-shouldered, Rothschild, blue-front, orange-wing, mealy and plain-colored.

The Best Amazon then competes for one of the four major parrot groups, in this case Best South American Parrot. Other categories include Best Macaw, Best South

Ruffled feathers do not win points at a bird show. Fortunately, these Cuban Amazons are not on exhibition—they're sleeping.

American Parakeet, Best Conure, Best *Pionus* and Best Caique.

If an Amazon is selected Best South American Parrot, it is then eligible to compete against the Best South Pacific, Best Afro-Asian and Best Mutation Parrot for Best Parrot In Show. An Amazon that makes it all the way is then eligible for Supreme Best In Show in competition with Best Canary, Best Finch, Best Dove, Best Softbill and Best Mule or Hybrid. It is a gradual elimination contest until one bird emerges the over-all victor.

A show bird must be familiar with moving from its perch to the judge's stick—in much the same way as this tamed yellow-naped confidently moves from wrist to hand.

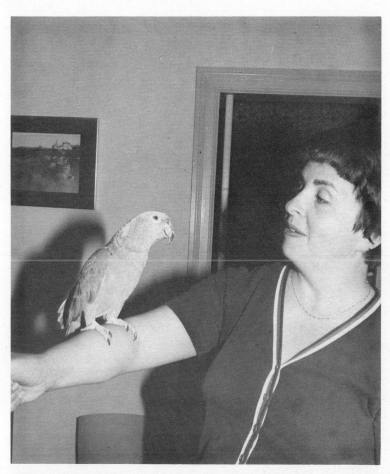

A bird will be faulted in competition if it is not steady on the perch. Here, practice includes perching on the owner's arm.

In preparing your bird for show, you should cage it in preparation three to four weeks before the show so it is completely at home on its perch. Work with it with a pointer so it will be familiar with a judge's stick. Make sure that no wing or tail feathers are damaged. Damaged feathers will pull down a bird quite badly in competition. I would urge every pet owner and aviculturist to exhibit. It is fun.

To successfully breed Amazons, you should first be sure that your birds are a true pair and are at least five years old; they also must be in good health. Pictured here is a Cuban Amazon, an Amazon now being successfully bred in captivity.

Chapter 5
Breeding the Amazon

Once you have successfully bred an Amazon, you have reached star status in the world of aviculture. Of all the parrots, Amazon parrots definitely are among the most difficult to breed in captivity.

It may sound as if I'm belaboring the obvious, but the first step in the successful breeding of Amazons is to start off with a true pair. Too frequently a breeder finds he has two males or two females after three, four or five years of trying. Today, with the aid of the endoscope and other similar devices, one has benefits not offered to aviculturists in the past. Secondly, even after you're sure you have a true pair, you have to be very sure of their age. This is important, because in my experience I have found that there is no Amazon that breeds under five years of age. As a matter of fact, most of the Amazons that I have had the good fortune of successfully breeding have been known to be much older than five years of age. One pair of Panama Amazons that bred for me were about fifteen and ten years old, respectively. When an aviculturist has a true pair of Amazons and both are over five years of age, *then* perhaps he can think of the necessities that go with breeding.

It has often been said that you should select a large, quiet area for the best breeding conditions for your birds. This is sometimes true, but at other times it depends entirely on the birds themselves and the situation in which they exist. We had a pair of Amazons that loved people so much that they preferred a breeding aviary in which plenty of people would bother them. I do not particularly condone this—but on the other hand, the birds did successfully breed and raise chicks through much confusion. Generally, however, it is best to select an aviary about six feet long, five feet wide and seven feet high in a quiet area. It is also best to keep strangers and visitors that are semi-strangers away, since some Amazons are bothered with their nesting activities. I have heard that some Amazons have left their nest during visits from strangers to their aviary.

I have also seen Amazons breed in small cages. One pair of yellow-naped Amazons laid two eggs and incubated them on the floor of a large monkey cage. One egg hatched, according to the owner; the parents treated it with care and were successful in raising this baby to adulthood.

Apparently, the answer is that all conditions vary; surprisingly, what works well for me may not work well for you, but I'll give you my recommendations as a general guide. Ideally, the nest box should be large, dark and roomy and should have a good entrance. The nest must have security. It is best to place good black greenhouse dirt or soil on the bottom of the nest box. This can be covered with a few shavings. We have found that with this type of material in the nest bottom there is sufficient moisture for the Amazons.

We have always allowed the parent birds to feed and care for the young Amazons, but there are many excellent breeders who feed the young by hand with very good results. Most certainly they end up with a very tame baby or babies. We feed several treats to the parents when they are busily feeding their young. Our favorite (and theirs) is bread, preferably whole dark wheat, and milk. Cheese, corn on the cob and various fruits are also readily taken. Canned baby foods, including plums and oatmeal with bananas and apple sauce, are the favorites.

It must be understood that a tame parrot will make just as

An ideal breeding aviary for Amazons should be large, have nest boxes which are roomy and will provide security, and be situated in a quiet area. This aviary is in a basement.

It generally takes about 28 days for Amazon eggs to hatch. *Below:* the hand-feeding of this double yellow-head will probably result in a very tame baby bird.

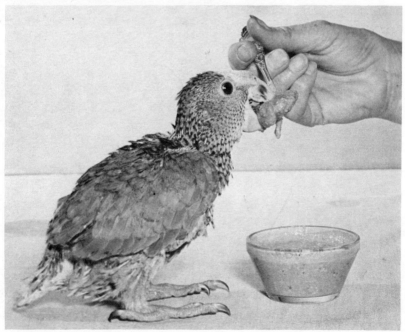

These seven-week-old double yellow-head Amazons exhibit the black toenails and tongues typical of baby yellow-heads. These will change to flesh-color as the babies mature. More yellow will appear on the head after about eight months.

good a breeder as one that is wild. The major difference involves nastiness when brooding; because the tame parrot is not afraid of a human it will be more domineering and dangerous when involved in breeding. The wild Amazon will still be somewhat afraid of the human even when incubating and feeding the young.

Although the vinaceous Amazon is on the list of endangered Amazon parrots, it might soon be reclassified as threatened rather than endangered.

Chapter 6
The Endangered Amazons

Certain regulations issued by the Department of the Interior implement the Convention on International Trade in Endangered Species of Wild Fauna and Flora.

There are eight endangered Amazon parrots at present. I shall discuss those eight species in the order of rarity and danger of extinction.

Perhaps the most acutely endangered is the Puerto Rican Amazon, *Amazona vittata,* which exists only on the island of Puerto Rico. It is so rare that the total number of birds listed in the world numbers from 15 to 30. Very few people in the future will ever see the Puerto Rican Amazon; very few people today, in fact, will be lucky enough to see the Puerto Rican Amazon. Unfortunately, unless active environmental work is accomplished, this bird will become extinct.

The Department of the Interior covers the species *Amazona leucocephala* as one entity; consequently all five subspecies are listed as endangered. This includes the Cuban, the Isle of Pines Amazon, the Grand Cayman Amazon, the Cayman Brac Amazon and the Bahaman Amazon. Of the five, the rarest seems to be the Bahaman Amazon, with supposedly fewer than two hundred restricted to only one island off the Bahamas. The Cayman Brac Amazon appears to be less rare but still with no more than six hundred left on Little Cayman and Cayman Brac islands. A native of

Jamaica told me that there are at least a thousand Isle of Pines Amazons remaining on the Isle of Pines. This little island is just southwest of Cuba. Close friends who visit Grand Cayman island have studied the Grand Cayman Amazon and state that there are fewer than two thousand remaining. Recent discussions with Cubans, however, reveal that the Cuban Amazon is still common in certain forests of Cuba. They believe that certain subspecies of *A. leucocephala,* such as the Cuban, should be classified as threatened rather than endangered. Fortunately there are two or three very successful breeders who are specializing in *Amazona leucocephala* subspecies. They are to be commended on the fine breeding successes they have achieved.

The St. Vincent Amazon, *Amazona guildingii,* is classified properly as gravely endangered. We believe, from personal visits to the island of St. Vincent, that there are fewer than five hundred Amazons left on that volcanic island. We understand that at least two United States zoos and a trust on the island of Jersey in the British Isles are successfully breeding the St. Vincent. We wish them continued great success.

The grand imperial Amazon, *Amazona imperialis,* from the island of Dominica, is classified as endangered. No one seems to know just how many remain. My guess is about five hundred to a thousand. Perhaps the most beautiful of all the Amazons, the imperial is seldom seen, and there are no successful breeding colonies in captivity.

Amazona versicolor, the St. Lucia Amazon, is also endangered. Living only on the island of St. Lucia in the Antilles, this rare Amazon is found only in the deep interiors. Reports from native St. Lucians show that several hundred to a thousand Amazons still exist. It is unfortunate that hunters are the greatest danger to these birds. A similar problem exists in Dominica for the Imperial and the St. Vincent on St. Vincent island. I am horrified whenever a native tells me how delicious parrot soup tastes!

If aviculturists were allowed to obtain and breed the endangered Amazons, these birds might be as plentiful in captivity as the once endangered turquoisine parakeet shown here.

The red-spectacled Amazon, *Amazona pretrei pretrei,* is considerably rare in the Amazon forests of Brazil and Uruguay. Forest clearing and penetration of the forests by civilization make the true spectacled Amazon quite endangered.

Of the two remaining, the vinaceous Amazon, *Amazona vinacea,* and *Amazona dufresniana rhodocorytha,* the red-crowned Amazon (which Interior calls the red-browed Amazon, *Amazona rhodocorythia*), I believe both are more common than various aviculturists and ornithologists originally thought. Perhaps within the near future these species will be reclassified as only threatened instead of endangered.

We believe that aviculturists will save various endangered species if allowed to breed and reproduce them, as has been done with the turquoisine parakeet, the Swinhoe pheasant and the Bali mynah. These three birds, thanks to the breeding expertise of aviculturists, are now plentiful in captivity. Breeders of the Nene goose brought it back from near extinction. Today this Hawaiian goose is being released back into the wild.

Aviculturists should be allowed to breed specific endangered and threatened species. Many aviculturists have successfully bred certain species that zoos and research facilities have failed to reproduce. Finally, various laws and regulations that prohibit the interstate exchange of good endangered breeding stock can only be detrimental to the final need—that is, the continuance and thriving future of the endangered species.

Chapter 7
Preventive Medicine

One always wants to prevent the occurrence of diseases and parasite infestations in cage and aviary birds. Preventive medicine is most important; if followed correctly one can achieve standards that will save much stress and suffering in the future.

The most important aspect of preventive medicine deals with the acquisition of new birds; one must always isolate new birds for *at least* thirty days, and sixty would be better. During the isolation period, one must watch for signs of distress, weakness and poor appetite.

It is always wise to immediately start utilizing a high-protein, high-vitamin diet. We suggest the addition of vitamins to the diet. Aviculturists can feel fortunate, since certain commercial forms of multi-vitamin preparations are available; these preparations provide the necessary A-B-C-D and E vitamins.

Vitamin A is required for the normal development of bone structure, but in the new cagebird it is especially valuable in building immunity against certain diseases. For this reason, giving extra vitamin A according to directions is advisable with new birds. Vitamin A is unstable, so it is important not to depend upon its provision in a food that has been stored for a long time; the vitamin A content would have disappeared. We suggest feeding a good supply of apples and carrots for vitamin A provision.

Vitamin D aids in the absorption and disposition of

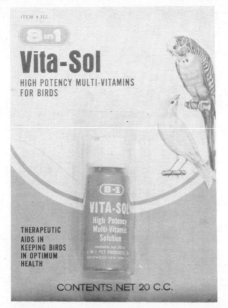

Since vitamins and minerals are very important in a bird's diet, the use of supplements is highly recommended. The mineral block shown below also allows your bird to keep its beak trimmed.

calcium and phosphorus. A deficiency will cause rickets in young birds not receiving adequate vitamin D. Multivitamin supplements will help prevent rickets in young birds if you have success in hatching.

Vitamin E is important in the reproduction performance of the female Amazon and normal fertility in the mature male. Vitamin E should best be given to cagebirds in the form of multiple vitamins.

There are many vitamins in the *Vitamin B* complex; all are important in preventive medicine. Vitamin B is required for growth and hatchability. Amazons can readily receive plenty of B in multiple vitamins as well as whole wheat bread (which they seem to enjoy).

When you do buy birds we suggest that you select from a breeder first, particularly one who exhibits and has had long-standing breeding pairs. You will find that you are ahead, because it is a fact that breeder-produced birds are healthier.

Regardless of where you buy a bird, make sure the bird looks alert and not fluffed up. Stay away from a bird that constantly holds its head under its wing with fluffed up feathers. You may well be purchasing a sick bird that soon dies, and few sellers will replace a bird that you have had over two days.

Your prime sources of birds will be pet shops and private breeders. I believe that in the general run breeders will have healthier stock than pet shops, especially if the breeders have a long experience with birds. At the same time, many birds sold in pet shops have been obtained from private breeders and therefore share whatever advantages such stock offers. Additionally, not everyone can get into contact with a private breeder locally (there just aren't that many of them) and most people don't want to get mixed up with all the folderol they'd have to go through to purchase birds through the mails. All in all a private breeder might be your best source, but pet shops might be your only really *available* source.

When you add new birds it is best to isolate them in another home or building for the thirty to sixty days as previously mentioned. I would not do anything less.

Always watch the droppings of new birds. They should be solid green and white. If they become loose or yellowish green, you should go to an avian veterinarian immediately for advice and treatment.

If your bird gets fluffed up and listless, immediately place it in a high-heat area, preferably 90 degrees F.

With respiratory problems, before you go to a veterinarian specializing in avian diseases, place the recommended dosage of antibiotic powder in the drinking water. Use only tetracycline or achromycin. Do *not* use chloromycetin.

Sam, a plain-colored Amazon, enjoys a fine mist spray of water—a good method of bathing your bird.

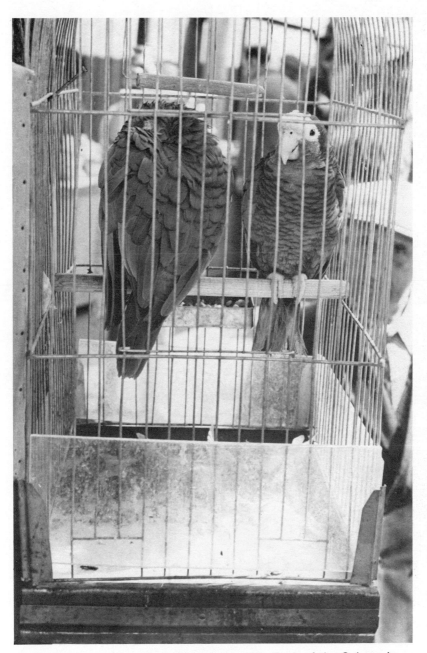

Crowding is not conducive to good health. Each of the Cubans in this pet store cage has ruffled feathers.

This sick yellow-naped Amazon is in a hospital cage which is equipped with a cover and a light for extra warmth. Hand-feeding of such a bird will ensure that proper medication and nourishment will be taken by the bird.

Another wonder drug that has proved successful for me is the use of Vicks Vapor Rub on the nostrils. Keep in mind that in preventive medicine you may have to use some medicine. You should view your Amazon at least three times per day for any changes in the bird's disposition, ruffled or fluffed up feathers, drowsiness, restlessness, pasty vent area, loss of appetite and abnormal droppings. These changes should be apparent immediately, and with luck you will keep your Amazon from illness for years.

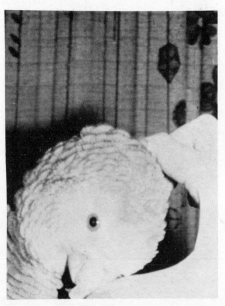

While this Rothschild's Amazon is having her head scratched, her owner can closely examine the bird for signs of ill health. *Below:* there are many medications available to help cure a sick bird.

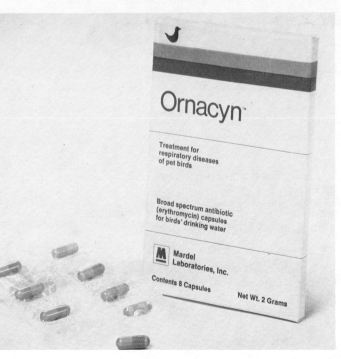

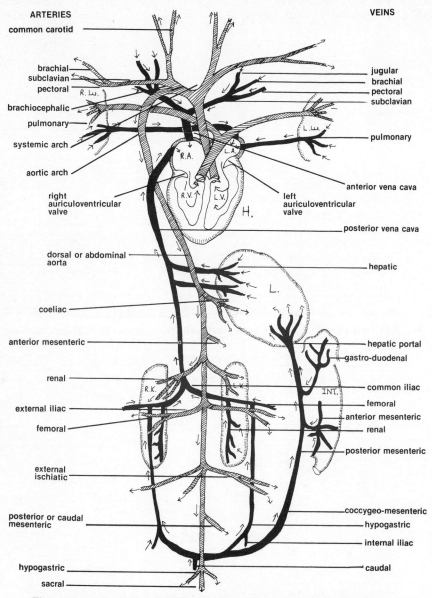

ARTERIES

common carotid

brachial
subclavian
pectoral

brachiocephalic

pulmonary

systemic arch

aortic arch

right
auriculoventricular
valve

dorsal or abdominal
aorta

coeliac

anterior mesenteric

renal

external iliac

femoral

external
ischiatic

posterior or caudal
mesenteric

hypogastric

sacral

VEINS

jugular
brachial
pectoral
subclavian

pulmonary

anterior vena cava

posterior vena cava

hepatic

hepatic portal
gastro-duodenal

common iliac
femoral
anterior mesenteric
renal

posterior mesenteric

coccygeo-mesenteric
hypogastric
internal iliac

caudal

left
auriculoventricular
valve

R. Lu.   L. Lu.
R.A.   L.A.
R.V.   L.V.   H.
L.
R.K.   L.K.   INT.

The arrows show the direction of blood flow in the cardiovascular
system of a bird. R.Lu. = right lung; L.Lu. = left lung; R.A. = right
auricle; L.A. = left auricle; R.V. = right ventricle; L.V. = left ventricle; H. = heart; L. = liver; R.K. = right kidney; L.K. = left kidney;
INT. = intestine. (Drawing by Janet Keymer)

Chapter 8
Common Ailments and Diseases Affecting Amazons

You may recall that we discussed the great importance of warmth as an essential element necessary in the treatment of a sick bird. Remember that when a bird is sick, the minimum temperature to use is 85 degrees F. Any sick bird should be housed and given treatment in this heat until it has recovered. At that time only should the temperature be gradually reduced.

Here are some of the most common ailments of Amazon parrots.

Vitamin Deficiency

Small yellow pustules will occur in the mouth, and on a lost bird these yellow pustules will be seen on autopsy of the esophagus. Treat with Vitamin A as soon as pustules appear. You should add multi-vitamins to an Amazon's diet at all times to prevent occurrences such as this.

Aspergillosis

This is caused by a fungus called *Aspergillus fumigatu* which invades the throat and the air sacs and lungs of the bird. Prevention is by feeding only clean seed. Don't let the seed get moldy. There is no completely adequate treatment once a bird has this disease. Do not use moldy hay or straw. This is a carrier of the organism. Amazons with this disease

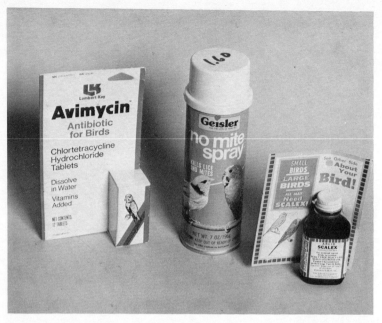

Your local pet shop carries several lines of bird products which will help maintain a healthy bird, cure a sick bird and/or prevent problems from occurring.

make a wheezing sound when breathing. They appear to have deep and severe respiratory difficulty.

Bumblefoot

This results in Amazons from a *Staphylococcus* infection. Drainage and then treatment with antibiotics will be successful. Bumblefoot most frequently occurs in Amazons recently imported and kept in congregated flocks while in quarantine.

Bronchitis

Serious nasal discharge occurs, accompanied by a severe respiratory difficulty. The Amazon becomes depressed and fluffs its feathers. The bird will eat fairly well during this bad period. Treat with terramycin or aureomycin in water.

Spray with cortisone in nostrils. Also apply Vicks Vapor Rub on nostrils. Place in heat as usual. You may also unplug nostrils with a toothpick and steam with melted Vicks thirty minutes per day.

Cataracts

This is a hereditary disease of the eyes, carried by a dominant gene. It is best to dispose of breeders that produce young in which cataracts are prevalent. Fortunately, this is not seen often in Amazons.

Chills

If taken to warmth in time, almost all birds with simple chill will definitely recover within twelve hours if put in a temperature of 85 to 90 degrees F.

Convulsions

On occasion, one will see an Amazon in a convulsion. Almost always the convulsion is associated with a Vitamin B deficiency. Prevent it first by administering the liquid multi-vitamins. Two mg. of thiamine HCL daily will prevent further convulsions.

Conjunctivitis

This condition occurs as a watery discharge from the eye, and the eyelids may become swollen to the extent that temporary blindness occurs. Immediately apply an antibiotic ointment containing an approved antibiotic. Do not use streptomycin, which is dangerous to birds.

Constipation

Fortunately this condition does not often occur in Amazons, but when it does, you must try to feed greens, particularly cabbage and lettuce. Two drops of castor oil can also be given by mouth.

Crop Binding

This occurs in young Amazons more often than in adults. You should manipulate the crop to dislodge the binding. Give mineral oil by mouth; this will ease the dislodged material to the lower esophagus into the proventriculus and on to the gizzard.

Crop Sickness

A bird with crop sickness vomits a watery fluid from the beak continuously. You must distinguish this behavior from normal actions between breeding Amazons. Acute cases can be treated with Kaopectate or bicarbonate of soda. Do not feed any gravel for a few days.

Egg Binding

Egg binding is caused by constriction of the oviduct and goes along with cold weather or sudden changes in temperature. Amazon hens usually come off the nest and sit in a corner all fluffed up. The wings are dropped and the eyes are closed. In most cases complete recovery will occur if you place the bird in 90 degree heat. In just a few hours the egg will be laid. Hens that become egg-bound should be rested for at least sixty days. A prevention has worked for this author: give one teaspoonful of gin in a half pint of water while birds are laying.

Enteritis

This is actually an inflammation of the intestines. Causes are many; it could have a psychological cause such as extreme nervousness and excitement. Changes in diet or environment will also cause enteritis. Vascular blood changes within the intestine will also cause enteritis. It might also have a nutritional cause, such as too much fruit, too many greens, deficiency of grit or coprophagy, which is the eating of other bird's droppings. Various infections will cause enteritis. Some of the worst are those caused by

This diseased yellow-fronted Amazon exhibits clenched feet, lordosis (forward curvature of the spine) and opisthotonus (backward curvature of the neck).

Salmonella, Pasteurella and *Streptococcus.* Symptoms include abnormal green and watery droppings which may be bloody. The feathers are ruffled and the Amazon is listless. Affected birds often have a pasty vent and wet feathers.

When you treat you should consider all types of enteritis to be infectious. Treat with broad-spectrum antibiotics such as terramycin or aureomycin. B-complex vitamins are also necessary as well as additional fluids. Other home treatments include boiled rice water, which is extremely helpful. You can also boil three teabags for five minutes, let them steep and then let the Amazons drink after the tea has cooled somewhat.

When studying the droppings of Amazons with enteritis you should pay attention to the following colors and conditions:

Yellow to yellow green—infectious
brown, dry scanty—pneumonia
yellow with blood—psittacosis
grayish white and watery—coccidiosis
gray and gummy—nephritis or kidney disease

Impacted Gizzard

Symptoms are similar to those of enteritis. Treat with increased fluid intake with two or four drops of mineral oil.

Indigestion

This condition can be related to the above. It often occurs from too much grit or gravel, which causes irritation of the intestine by overflowing through to the gizzard. The remedy is to remove the gravel and the condition will subside. Sometimes Amazons will ingest too much sunflower seed. Certain Amazons will stuff themselves and suffer later.

Overgrown Beak

Often in older Amazons the upper mandible grows too long and often becomes distorted. It also may cross the lower mandible. You must take great care in trimming the beak. The best instrument is the dog toenail clipper in conjunction with a sharp pair of scissors.

Overgrown Claws

Luckily this condition does not always affect the Amazon. If the condition does occur, you can hold the claw in a good light and cut it—very carefully—with dog toenail clippers. Make sure you clip *below* the blood vessel. Once in a while you might get a bleeder; if you do, you're in trouble. If bleeding occurs, use flour on the claw. If it continues to bleed, secure the services of a veterinarian experienced in avian problems.

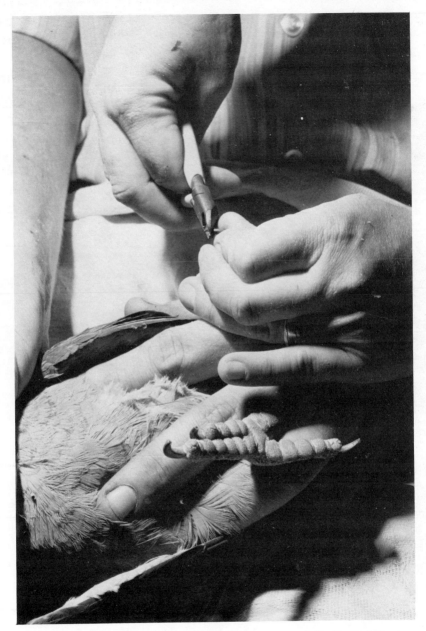

Clipping your bird's claws must be done very carefully. It would be a good idea to have two people to do the job: one to hold the bird and one to clip the claws.

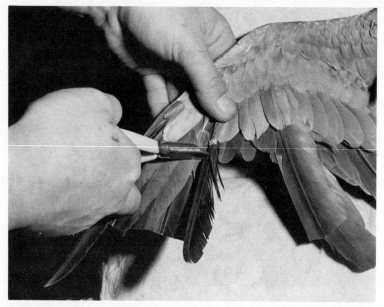

If your Amazon is to be flightless, one wing must be trimmed of all but three flight feathers at the end of the wing. This operation, however, must be done by an experienced bird owner or a veterinarian. It is very important that the blood feathers not be cut.

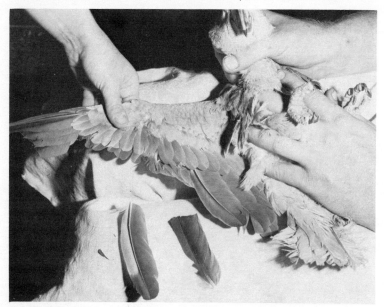

Pneumonia

This often occurs as a result of a chill or a draft. If left unattended your Amazon will surely die. You should *immediately* place the bird in your hospital cage at a temperature of 90 degrees F. Give one teaspoon of whiskey and one teaspoon of a liquid sulfa drug about every four hours. We have saved some birds this way. Do not give a sulfa drug any more than three successive days to an Amazon.

Scabies

We once saw a colony of Amazons very much infested with a parasitic mite. These birds had been attacked around the beak and legs and appeared to have an extra horny growth, with much scabbiness and bleeding from chewing. Furacin ointment has been used on this condition with success. The parasitic mite causing this condition is *Cnemidocoptes mutans*.

Mites are arachnids which often parasitize birds. These microscopic parasites are troublesome, but they can be prevented and/or successfully treated.

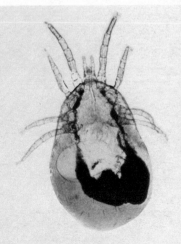

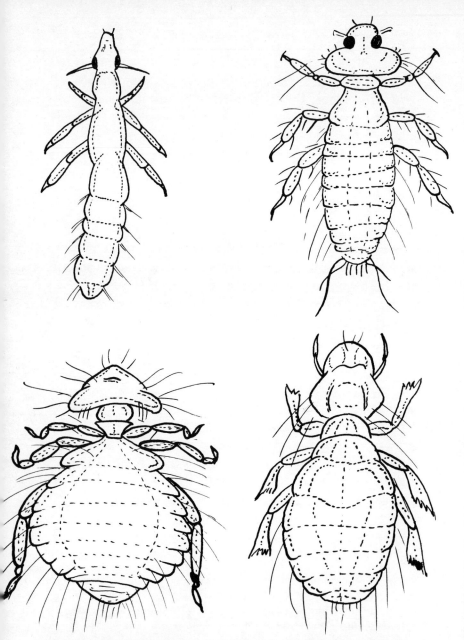

Bird lice are small, wingless insects which live as external parasites. Pictured here are the feather louse (upper left), the narrow body louse (upper right), the large body louse (lower left) and the golden feather louse (lower right). (Drawing by E. Weltz)

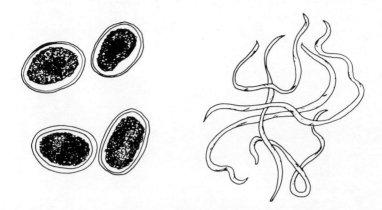

Roundworms are passed as eggs in infested birds' feces; the larvae develop into adult worms within a bird which ingests the eggs. Not drawn to scale. (Drawing by Janet Keymer)

Internal Parasites

Occasionally Amazons will develop internal roundworms. Roundworm ova can be detected in the droppings by microscopic study. Liquid piperazine is the drug of choice, two teaspoons to a half pint of water.

In summation you must consider the following:

1. Preventive measures will pay off.

2. If you notice that your bird is "off," place him in a heated area or a hospital cage with 85 to 90 degrees F. temperature.

3. My favorite treatments which have cured many birds are Vicks Vapor Rub on the nares and terramycin powder in the drinking water.

4. If you have real difficulty, consult your veterinarian. This writer has merely mentioned a few conditions seen in practice and experience in bird breeding populations.

Pacheco's disease affects all parrots—except conures. Conures seem to have a natural immunity to the disease, and they also appear to be carriers of it.

Chapter 9
Pacheco's Disease—
The Great Parrot Danger

•One summer day in 1977, a large western aviary noted an increased loss of cockatiels, perhaps seven or eight. An occasional loss of one was not unusual, but seven or eight was extraordinary. On the next day, an additional fifteen cockatiels were found dead. Before the episode was over, some 700 birds had died.

•In midwinter of the same year, an aviary in New England started losing Amazons in quantity. Within one week, they had lost over 50 Amazons, macaws and cockatoos.

•A large pet store in Massachusetts had purchased six Amazons from a broker; within one week not only the six Amazons but also all other parrots in the shop died rapidly.

In all cases a dread disease called Pacheco's disease was diagnosed. Today, this is the disease that you as aviculturists should fear. It is caused by a filterable virus which has been classified as a herpesvirus. There are many types of herpesviruses. One which you may all recognize causes fever blisters or cold sores about the mouth of humans. It is related to the dread Pacheco's disease virus.

Pacheco's disease was discovered by Dr. G. Pacheco during an epidemic of psittacosis (parrot fever) in man which occurred in the United States and Europe in 1929-1930. It was in Brazil that Dr. Pacheco and colleagues were working with sick and dead parrots. They discovered a new agent which was eventually classified as a virus that killed budgerigars in 3 to 5 days. Clinical manifestations of the budgerigars included ruffling of the feathers, progressive weakness, nasal discharge, diarrhea, loss of weight, nervous symptoms and almost immediate death.

Gross pathology consisted of necrotic areas of the liver and spleen. The important microscopic findings were demonstrated by the intranuclear inclusions in the liver cells. In 1975, Pacheco's disease was diagnosed in Florida in psittacine birds. It appears that the greatest danger involves conures, which tend to be inapparent carriers of the disease. To date there has been no effective vaccine produced to be used against the disease. Unsuccessful attempts to protect budgerigars by vaccinating them with a turkey herpesvirus have occurred; it is apparent that much work must be done to produce a good vaccine.

There can be much confusion in differentiating Pacheco's disease from viscerotropic velogenic Newcastle disease and psittacosis. In contrast to Pacheco's disease, VVND (Newcastle) can produce high mortality in young susceptible birds and produce swelling on the head and neck. Psittacosis shows more respiratory difficulties.

One should guard against adding any new birds directly into an aviary. It is recommended that an isolation of at least 60 days be imposed on any new birds. Any stress can cause a carrier bird to break out into active disease. Prophylactic treatment on susceptible birds includes continual dosing with B-complex vitamins. Chloramphenicol is the drug of choice for reduction of stress in birds that might be suspected as being carriers of Pacheco's disease.

If indeed you have birds that seem to have recovered from Pacheco's disease, you should recover blood serum from these birds, injecting it into any susceptible birds one week before adding them to the flock or aviary. This is a

It is important that you get to know your bird and its habits so that you will recognize any changes which might indicate a symptom of ill health. This orange-winged Amazon can be inspected while it sits on its owner's arm.

passive immunity that may add safety to aviaries until a natural immunity can be developed.

Pacheco's disease is the most dangerous threat today to the aviculturist and pet owner. Until such time as a vaccine is produced, each of us must be extremely cautious when adding birds to our aviaries.

The red-lored Amazon is one of the several species of Amazons which have successfully been bred in the United States.

THE SPECIES OF
AMAZON PARROTS

The fifty-six parrots which I classify as Amazon parrots are here listed alphabetically by their scientific name. Each entry tells the bird's common name(s), its geographic origin and its size in inches. Each Amazon will be discussed in detail following these brief descriptions.

Readers will no doubt notice that the listing as given here does not necessarily agree in every respect with the listing of species and subspecies as presented by other writers. Some of the birds that I have treated as subspecies, for example, might be treated by others as full species, and some that I have treated as full species are treated as subspecies in other works. Additionally, common names given here by me will not agree in every instance with the common names assigned by other authors, especially where those other authors are not Americans. And although I (as stated elsewhere in this book) feel that the hawkheaded parrot should be treated as an Amazon parrot as far as taxonomy is concerned, I have here listed it under its generally accepted scientific generic name of *Deroptyus* so that confusion can be avoided.

Amazona aestiva aestiva, (BLUE-FRONTED
  AMAZON):
  Brazil, Paraguay. 15 inches.
A. a. xanthopteryx, (YELLOW-WINGED AMAZON):
  Bolivia, Argentina. 15 inches.
A. agilis, (BLACK-BILLED AMAZON):
  Jamaica. 11 inches.
A. albifrons albifrons, (WHITE-FRONTED AMAZON):
  Mexico, Guatemala. 10 inches.
A. a. nana, (LESSER WHITE-FRONTED AMAZON):
  Mexico, Guatemala, Honduras, Belize, Costa Rica,
  Nicaragua. 9 inches.
A. a. saltuensis, (SONORA WHITE-FRONTED
  AMAZON):
  Mexico. 9 inches.
A. amazonica amazonica, (ORANGE-WINGED
  AMAZON):
  Colombia, Venezuela, Guyana, Surinam, Fr. Guiana,
  Brazil, Eduador, Panama. 13 inches.
A. a. tobagensis, (TOBAGO ORANGE-WINGED
  AMAZON):
  Trinidad, Tobago. 12 inches.
A. arausiaca, (RED-NECKED AMAZON):
  Island of Dominica. 17 inches.
A. autumnalis autumnalis, (RED-LORED AMAZON):
  Mexico, Honduras, Belize, Guatemala. 14 inches.
A. a. diadema, (DIADEMED AMAZON):
  Brazil. 14 inches.
A. a. lilacina, (LILACINE AMAZON):
  Ecuador. 13 inches.
A. a. salvini, (SALVIN'S AMAZON):
  Nicaragua, Costa Rica, Colombia. 14 inches.
A. barbadensis barbadensis, (YELLOW-SHOULDERED
  AMAZON):
  Venezuela, Island of Aruba. 13 inches.

A. b. rothschildi, (ROTHSCHILD'S AMAZON):
Venezuela, Island of Bonaire. 13 inches.

A. brasiliensis, (RED-TAILED AMAZON):
Brazil. 14 inches.

A. collaria, (YELLOW-BILLED AMAZON):
Jamaica. 12 inches.

A. dufresniana dufresniana, (BLUE-CHEEKED
AMAZON):
Guyana, Surinam. 14 inches.

A. d. rhodocorytha, (RED-CAPPED or RED-
CROWNED AMAZON):
Brazil. 14 inches.

A. farinosa farinosa, (MEALY AMAZON):
Venezuela, Guyana, Surinam. 16 inches.

A. f. guatemalae, (BLUE-CROWNED AMAZON):
Guatemala, Mexico, Honduras. 16 inches.

A. f. inornata, (PLAIN-COLORED AMAZON):
Panama, Venezuela, Colombia, Ecuador. 18 inches.

A. f. virenticeps, (GREEN-HEADED AMAZON):
Costa Rica, Panama. 14 inches.

A. festiva bodini, (BODIN'S AMAZON):
Venezuela, Guyana. 14 inches.

A. f. festiva, (FESTIVE AMAZON):
Ecuador, Peru. 14 inches.

A. finschi finschi, (FINSCH'S AMAZON):
Mexico. 12 inches.

A. f. woodi, (WOOD'S LILAC-CROWNED AMAZON):
Mexico. 12 inches.

A. guildingii, (ST. VINCENT AMAZON):
Island of St. Vincent. 18 inches.

A. imperialis, (IMPERIAL AMAZON):
Island of Dominica. 20 inches.

A. leucocephala bahamensis, (BAHAMAN AMAZON):
Bahama Islands. 13 inches.

A. l. caymanensis, (CAYMAN ISLAND AMAZON):
Grand Cayman Island, West Indies. 12 inches.

A. l. hesterna, (CAYMAN BRAC AMAZON):
Cayman Brac and Little Cayman, West Indies. 11 inches.

A. l. leucocephala, (CUBAN AMAZON):
Cuba, Isle of Pines. 13 inches.

A. l. palmarum, (ISLE OF PINES AMAZON):
Isle of Pines. 13 inches.

A. mercenaria canipalliata, (GRAY-NAPED AMAZON):
Bolivia. 13 inches.

A. m. mercenaria, (SCALY-NAPED AMAZON):
Venezuela, Ecuador, Bolivia. 13 inches.

A. ochrocephala auropalliata, (YELLOW-NAPED AMAZON):
Mexico, Costa Rica. 15 inches.

A. o. belizensis, (BELIZE AMAZON):
Belize. 12 inches.

A. o. magna, (MAGNA DOUBLE YELLOW-HEAD AMAZON):
Mexico. 18 inches.

A. o. nattereri, (NATTERER'S AMAZON):
Ecuador, Peru. 14 inches.

Sanchita, a Panama Amazon, shows how patriotic she is to her adopted homeland.

A. o. ochrocephala, (YELLOW-FRONTED AMAZON):
Colombia, Venezuela, Guyana, Surinam. 14 inches.

A. o. oratrix, (DOUBLE YELLOW-HEAD AMAZON):
Mexico. 15 inches.

A. o. panamensis, (PANAMA AMAZON):
Panama, Colombia. 12 inches.

A. o. parvipes, (SMALL YELLOW-NAPED AMAZON):
Honduras, Nicaragua. 12 inches.

A. o. tresmariae, (TRES MARIAS AMAZON):
Tres Marias Islands off Mexico. 16 inches.

A. o. xantholaema, (MARAJO YELLOW-HEADED
AMAZON):
Island of Marajo at mouth of Amazon. 14 inches.

A. pretrei, (RED-SPECTACLED AMAZON):
Brazil, Uruguay. 13 inches.

A. tucumana, (TUCUMAN AMAZON):
Argentina, Bolivia. 13 inches.

A. ventralis, (SANTO DOMINGO AMAZON):
Hispaniola. 12 inches.

A. versicolor, (ST. LUCIAN AMAZON):
Island of St. Lucia. 17 inches.

A. vinacea, (VINACEOUS AMAZON):
Brazil, Paraguay. 14 inches.

A. viridigenalis, (GREEN-CHEEKED or MEXICAN
RED HEAD AMAZON):
Mexico. 13 inches.

A. vittata, (PUERTO RICAN AMAZON):
Puerto Rico. 12 inches.

A. xantholora, (YELLOW-LORED AMAZON):
Mexico. 10 inches.

A. xanthops, (YELLOW-BELLIED AMAZON):
Brazil. 11 inches.

Deroptyus accipitrinus (HAWKHEADED PARROT):
Venezuela, Guyana, Surinam, Colombia, Brazil,
Ecuador, Peru. 14 inches.

BLUE-FRONTED AMAZON
Amazona aestiva aestiva

Perhaps one of the three most popular Amazons in the United States is the blue-fronted Amazon. Numerous households in this country possessing a parrot have a tame mimic called a blue-front as their pet.

More and more aviaries in the United States are attempting to breed the blue-front. It is a talented and mischievous bird. Several aviculturists with whom I am acquainted have selected fine pairs of blue-fronts for their basic breeding stock. There are few reports of successful breeding of the blue-fronted Amazon in the United States; aviculturists must apply themselves more frequently to successful breeding of not only blue-fronts but all other Amazons—all members of the parrot family, in fact.

As its name implies, this Amazon has a bright blue front; it also has a yellow crown, yellow about the eyes and lores to the ear coverts and down the throat. Some specimens I have seen have a yellow frontal band, with the remaining front and the forecrown a light blue; the crown and facial area are yellow. Still other specimens have a blue front, with blue extending to the lores and cheeks. Yellow ear

Opposite:
Several species of Amazons are found in Brazil. Pictured here is the region around the Araguaia River in central Brazil.

81

coverts and crown as well as throat are noted. I have seen numerous specimens in each category.

The nape and back are covered with green feathers, each edged in black. The bend of the wing is red, with some yellow in certain birds. In other blue-fronts, the yellow at the bend of the wing is non-existent. The primary wing feathers are blue, black and red. The tail is green, banded with yellow at the extreme ends. The base of the tail feathers shows much red. Breast and abdominal feathers are a lighter green with lessening black edges. The beak is a horny gray color.

We have several friends who own one or more blue-front Amazons. All of these friends praise the quality and quantity of speech created by this Amazon. One such fancier owns only one parrot, a blue-front, but he is a highly satisfied parrot owner. He has stated that if the blue-front he owns should die he would immediately search for and buy another blue-front. This particular bird calls the cat, meows like a cat, barks like a dog, growls like a dog and whistles a tune not one person can understand. In addition he carries on a conversation with the television. He loves to reiterate a few not-so-choice words which shouldn't be used around most people. He swears in Portuguese as well.

Another friend owns two blue-fronts. Time after time these two would be carrying on a conversation in Portuguese. Our friend thought it was a Spanish conversation until one day he employed a Portuguese plumber. The plumber had no idea our friend had any parrots. While he was working in the kitchen he could hear the most dramatic Portuguese conversation in the basement; his face became redder and redder until he insisted to the owner that he could not and would not work in a house where such things were going on. He indicated that the two people downstairs shouldn't be so loud and boisterous and so bold while other people are around. When my friend took the plumber downstairs the plumber was dumbfounded. He refuses to

Blue-fronted Amazon, *Amazona aestiva aestiva.*

this day to tell my friend what the pair of blue-fronts were saying, he'll say only that it was much too embarrassing even for the parrots to say. My friend from Ohio has the two blue-fronts to this day, and still they speak only Portuguese.

One Connecticut breeder now has ten pairs of blue-fronts housed in individual aviaries 10 x 10 x 8 feet. Each aviary has a 20-gallon garbage can which has a circular hole cut into the side approximately ten inches up from the bottom. These garbage cans are designed for nesting sites. Black peat and shavings are placed in the bottom for nesting cavities. (This nesting system is used often by the author.)

Our Connecticut friend strongly believes that his blue-front Amazons will soon be breeding. I feel that Amazons must be at least five years of age before they can effectively breed. They may copulate at an early age, but they will very seldom lay eggs and incubate them to full term before they are five years old. We have seen aviculturists who have indicated that their young Amazons were ready for breeding, but it usually turned out that the birds were not quite so young as originally thought. One should not become discouraged when year after year an Amazon pair will not breed.

Too often we note that breeding and show birds are increasing in popularity in macaws and in cockatoos; too infrequently, however, do we see breeding Amazons, and only slightly more often do we see show Amazons. All of us must attempt to breed the blue-front as well as all other Amazons. Hopefully, we will also see more well trained Amazons exhibited at the bird shows throughout the nation.

YELLOW-WINGED AMAZON
Amazona aestiva xanthopteryx

Several yellow-winged Amazons have been imported into this country as blue-fronts, and to this day there are hundreds of pet owners, pet stores and aviculturists who still do not realize they own a very rare subspecies of the true blue-fronted Amazon.

The greatest differentiating characteristic focuses on the bend of the wing; in the yellow-wing, as the name implies, the only color distinguished is yellow. You will recall that the true blue-front has much red at the bend of the wing.

The yellow on the head surrounds the eye, and the blue covers the entire front. On the skins I have studied, it is noted that the breast and abdomen feathers are a lighter green than in the blue-fronted Amazon.

I have seen several yellow-winged Amazons in various pet shops and aviaries and in private collections. To my knowledge, no yellow-winged Amazons have been successfully bred in the United States. However, since very few people know that they may have yellow-winged Amazons, it would be surprising to see records listed under the correct name.

BLACK-BILLED AMAZON
Amazona agilis

Often discussed as one of the rarest of Amazons, the black-billed Amazon is currently available at more than two import stations. A sudden increase in the bird's availability occurred, as over four hundred birds were imported from Jamaica in late 1978. Previous to this time, the black-billed

Amazon was never seen at aviaries or zoos in the United States.

Here is a solid, lustrous green Amazon with some red in the wings and a distinctive black bill; it was once thought to be close to extinction. It is found on the island of Jamaica, preferring the low forest areas: consequently it does not remain actively in the Blue Mountains or the John Crow Mountains of Jamaica.

The Jamaicans consider the black-billed Amazon a pest. It hinders pimiento farmers, since it thrives on the black seeds of the pimiento. This Amazon also loves ripe plantains and bananas.

The black-billed Amazon is basically a lustrous green with an abdomen of greenish yellow. The tail is a light yellowish green. Primary wing coverts are red; occasionally some of these coverts are green and red, but this is not indicative of sex differentiation. Primary feathers are purplish blue; secondaries are dark blue and green. The striking characteristic is the black bill, which becomes darker at the base.

Since this species had not been imported except for an occasional pet bird importation prior to 1978, little is known of its breeding habits in captivity. Prior to 1978, I had seen only a few birds in the markets of Jamaica. Natives would remove babies from hollow nests and hand-feed them with moist banana. A few would be listed for sale at the farmers' markets.

One extremely interesting and intelligent Jamaican told me an interesting yarn concerning his favorite black-billed Amazon, named "Green Pepper." He personally went into the forest to look for baby parrots each season in order to sell them at the markets. He would climb trees and select those babies big enough to hand-feed with a combination of banana and cooked rice chewed to a proper consistency in his mouth.

In one nest were three partially feathered babies, one

about twice the size of the other two—and later to be twice as much of a piggy as the other two. This bird was destined to become Green Pepper. Inevitably, Green Pepper would become a glutton upon receiving his banana and rice diet. Green Pepper's great joy was to regurgitate with an attempt at feeding our Jamaican friend.

When it came time to bring the nearly twenty birds to market, Green Pepper was by far the largest and fattest. It was thought that surely he would be sold first. However, time after time he was passed over for smaller and cuter parrots. In due time, all the parrots were sold except Green Pepper. Our Jamaican friend decided to retain Green Pepper as his mascot. Year after year this duo sold not only young parrots at the farmers' market, but yams and green peppers as well. The green peppers were the vegetable type, though—not an apparently still-gluttonous parrot.

It is my understanding that this pair still exists in the Jamaican markets. If you get down there, look for them.

WHITE-FRONTED AMAZON
Amazona albifrons albifrons

Perhaps no other Amazon parrot species is more abundant in aviculture than *Amazona albifrons,* the species encompassing the three subspecies known as the white-fronted Amazon, the lesser white-fronted Amazon and the Sonora. In addition, probably no other Amazon parrot is more frequently improperly named than the birds of this species. In fact, these birds are so frequently called "spectacled" Amazons that that name is now readily acceptable terminology. Confusion results, because another Amazon also is known by a commonly accepted popular name that includes the word "spectacled"; this is the red-spectacled

Amazon, *Amazona pretrei*. A friend of mine once went through an ordeal in ordering a pair of red-spectacled Amazons. He wanted to receive and thought that he would receive *Amazona pretrei*, but when his birds arrived it was evident that a small but cute pair of white-fronted Amazons had been shipped instead. The difference in value was considerable, as the white-fronteds are much cheaper than the red-spectacled Amazon (and although the shipper did not make good on his error, my friend took care of him in a later deal.)

The general plumage is green, with posterior crown and nape having black edging on each feather. This black edging carries down the entire back. The front and forecrown are white. The lores and the entire area about the eye are bright red. The crown is blue. The alula of the wing of the male is red; the red is absent in the female. Consequently, here is one Amazon that is sexually dimorphic. Primary coverts are red, while primary and secondary feathers of the wing are green and blue. There is red at the base of the tail. The tips of the tail, as well as the tail coverts, are yellowish green.

The white-fronted Amazon has been successfully bred and raised in this country on numerous occasions. A close friend in Rhode Island has a very tame white-fronted Amazon called "Spec." This bird loves the man of the house but severely attacks both ladies of the household. For some reason, the sight of a woman infuriates "Spec." It could be that this bird had no connection or physical contact with a woman before being domesticated; therefore he does not like them now. However, most people would theorize that somewhere in the past a woman was mean or extremely strict with the bird.

Spec loves to fly onto ladies' heads and search for ears to bite. She has been known to inflict a painful bite. Yet strange men can visit this private home and, of course, Spec is a sweet, lovable thing. We theorize that female parrots seem to tolerate men better than women, and, in contrast, male parrots prefer women. This is not always a fact but holds true in general.

My son Daren has owned "Pinero," a white-fronted Amazon, for several years. Daren simply has to snap his fingers and Pinero will fly to perch on his shoulders. Pinero's favorite food is a small chunk of fresh coconut. He will turn over and play dead, and he'll roll over and over for a taste of coconut. Once he has had his fill, he wouldn't perform on a bet. After feeding, one of Pinero's favorite tricks is to bite fingers—except for Daren. This bird loves Daren so much that he will attack anyone who threatens or attempts to hit Daren. Needless to say, Daren gets hit in fun many times just to irritate Pinero.

Those fanciers who have bred the white-fronted Amazon report to me that they will lay as many as four eggs per nesting. As the new imports grow older, perhaps many more nestings will occur, but it is doubtful that an Amazon under five years of age will actually reproduce.

LESSER WHITE-FRONTED AMAZON
Amazona albifrons nana

Within the three subspecies of *Amazona albifrons, A. albifrons nana* is imported least frequently into the United States. It is readily imported, but only about one-third as many are seen as of the white-fronted Amazon (*A.a. albifrons*) and the Sonora white-fronted Amazon (*A.a. saltuensis*).

Perhaps the most notable instance of sexual dimorphism in Amazon parrots occurs in this subspecies: the female has hardly any white front, whereas the male has a considerable white frontal area. Both sexes have the usual red lores and red about the eyes. The crown is green which extends to the nape; each feather is edged with a dusky black. This subspecies occurs naturally in Central America, particularly Nicaragua and Guatemala.

This subspecies has been successfully bred in the United States. One breeder in New York, a lady with a flair for breeding parrots, has a pair that are seven years of age. She purchased a pair in Honduras when they were nestlings. During this seven-year period they were inseparable. They were always interested in food but never the nest box, which was added to their environment when they were three years of age. Finally, at the age of seven, they both spent a great deal of time in the nest. On peeking, the lady counted four eggs. All hatched in what appeared to be four weeks. She removed them all and fed them by hand. Consequently she had four of the tamest, most fascinating baby Amazons anyone could want. She liked them all so very much that she decided to keep all four.

SONORA WHITE-FRONTED AMAZON
Amazona albifrons saltuensis

One of the most frequently imported Amazons is the Sonora white-fronted, *Amazona albifrons saltuensis*. All of the *A. albifrons* subspecies are readily imported, but the Sonora makes its way into the homes of United States pet owners in great numbers.

Typically, the Sonora white-fronted Amazon lives up to its name; it has an extensive white front, with a dark bluish mauve crown extending to the nape of the neck. An extensive area of the breast has a bluish color. The lower abdomen is green; each feather lacks the usual black edging. The lores and area about the eyes are bright red. The primary wing coverts or alula are red in the male. The first primary feather is black; the next four are green at the base, with increasing blue towards the tips. The secondaries are blue. Tail feathers are yellowish green, with bright yellow green at the tips. Lateral feathers are green with red bases.

A potential parrot owner who wants an Amazon that is somewhat quiet should select this subspecies. In my experience, after viewing many Sonora white-fronted, white-fronted and lesser white-fronted Amazons, it is noteworthy to mention that the Sonora subspecies is exceptionally quiet. They do not screech like most other Amazons. Sonora white-fronted Amazons are easily sexed by the color of primary coverts; the males are bright and heavily red.

We see many *Amazona albifrons* individuals at the eastern shows. Most of the winners selected seem to be Sonora white-fronteds. Evidently the blue shadings on the head and breast bring out a contrast which seems to please the judges to a greater extent. This added color is not seen in *A.a. albifrons* and *A.a. nana*.

In one bird show in which over 200 parrots were exhibited, all three white-fronted subspecies were represented. All were in competition in the same class, but only the best one went on to compete with all other Amazons for Best Amazon. The most quiet, the smallest and currently the least expensive of the Amazons, the Sonora white-fronted Amazon is a good choice as a companion and a pet.

Orange-winged Amazon, *Amazona amazonica amazonica.*

ORANGE-WINGED AMAZON
Amazona amazonica amazonica

A smaller Amazon than the blue-front, the orange-winged Amazon has a more distinctive squared-off but pointed tail when the tail is closed; a distinct orange color in the wings and in the tail also is typical of the orange-winged Amazon. With familiarity, even at a distance, one can easily distinguish the orange-wing from the blue-fronted Amazon. Yet too often the orange-wing is called a blue-front. The front and lores are light blue; this blue extends above the eye, while the crown is yellow. Wing feathers are orange, black, blue and green. The secondaries have an orange speculum on three feathers. The green feathers of the nape are edged with black. Tail feathers are green with orange bases.

Many orange-winged Amazons have been imported into the United States in the last few years; in 1977 there were close to 3000 imported into the Los Angeles area alone, yet the orange-wing was ranked only eighth in number among the Amazons imported into the country that year. At the eastern bird shows it is indicative that orange-wing Amazons are leaders of all Amazon entries and possibly all parrots. They are extremely popular.

I have had orange-wings for several years. Although they are not the best of talkers, they do rival all other Amazons for their antics. Pinto is a cute and small orange-wing in our aviaries. He loves apple above all other foods; he will always take apple from my hands.

Pinto is cautious around strangers but is especially endearing to members of our family. He prefers a Santo Domingo Amazon over other orange-wings and has selected this bird for his mate. When we remove Pinto from his aviary, the Santo Domingo attacks with much haste.

As mentioned previously, the orange-wing is numerous at

bird shows. The quality of the birds shown is so consistent that their class is one of the most difficult to judge. I once judged a class of fifteen orange-wings; at least six were outstanding, rather steady and with good feather and color. At lesser shows each of these six could have gone on to Best Amazon. With some difficulty they were correctly placed. Because they are smaller than most other Amazons, orange-wings are not among the favorites of most aviculturists. It would be pleasant to see more aviculturists get involved in breeding this attractive species.

TOBAGO ORANGE-WINGED AMAZON
Amazona amazonica tobagensis

The only major difference morphologically between *A.a. amazonica* and *A.a. tobagensis* occurs in the wing secondaries. In the Tobago orange-wing the orange speculum occurs on four secondaries, while in the nominate subspecies the speculum occurs only on three secondaries.

Although most of the orange-wing Amazons come from Colombia, Venezuela and the Guianas, an occasional group comes from Trinidad and Tobago. Because of this difference in range, it is important to note the differentiating characteristics of each subspecies. We believe that the true orange-wing Amazon was brought to the islands of Trinidad and Tobago by traders.

Most aviculturists do not know how to distinguish these subspecies. Perhaps if you have one or more orange-wings in your collection you should check them out to see whether you have members of different subspecies.

RED-NECKED AMAZON
Amazona arausiaca

In my travels throughout the Caribbean and specifically to the island of Dominica in the West Indies, I was horrified to find that the rare and infrequently seen red-necked Amazon was still hunted for food by natives. Parrot soup is quite a delicacy in Dominica. What a shame! Not only is the exceptionally rare red-necked Amazon sparsely found on Dominica but the imperial Amazon also is rare on that island.

In discussions with native Dominicans, I was told that in certain forests there are still many red-necked Amazons. Surprisingly, natives only know how to shoot parrots. Natives in other jungle forests have learned to cut down trees to obtain nestlings from their hollow nests. The red-necked Amazon is in greatest danger because it prefers the lowlands, where hunters put it in grave danger.

In my travels, I was able to locate a few red-necked Amazons along the Picard and Barry Rivers not too far from Portsmouth. On the other side of the island, it was overwhelming to see a group of about a dozen red-necked Amazons flying along the Yellow River.

In viewing the few red-necked Amazons which I was fortunate enough to observe, I noted that some of them had little or no red on their necks. I am certain that these were juvenile birds. It is apparent that as they develop in age they show an increase in red about the neck. In the adults, the general plumage is green. The feathers of the nape and lower back of the neck are green edged in black. The front, forecrown, lores and upper cheeks, as well as the entire immediate area around the lower mandible, are brilliant violet blue; a blending of green feathers with scatterings of blue edges occur in the lower cheek areas. The ventral part of the neck is bright crimson red. Primary coverts of the wing are dark green; primaries are dark green, becoming violet blue. The outer three (sometimes four) secondaries are red extending to yellow, then blue. Fourth and fifth secondaries appear yellowish, ending with blue. The tail is green tipped with yellowish green. The bill is horn-colored and the legs are gray.

A close friend in Pennsylvania has been owned by two lovely red-necked Amazons for over twenty years. I truthfully believe the Amazons and humans both are fully dedicated to each other. Unfortunately both birds are apparently males. This is too bad, since breeding pairs are rare. Hopefully, trusts will be set up for the Amazons and the parrot world similar to the trusts that exist today for waterfowl, rare pheasants and cranes over the world. Only through these methods will the red-necked and other rare Amazons be saved.

RED-LORED AMAZON
Amazona autumnalis autumnalis

The red-lored Amazon, also called the yellow-cheeked Amazon, is indeed a devoted pet when tamed. We owned Pedro, a red-lored Amazon, for several years. We believe Pedro was unusually old when we traded for him. He was mischievous; he loved to screech and thoroughly enjoyed imitating the wolf whistle. When we obtained Pedro in trade for a pygmy goat, he was an ardent feather-picker. Time and energy as well as attention changed this state of affairs, and soon Pedro had a bright new set of feathers. Pedro, like all other red-lored Amazons, had a forehead of bright red. The lores are also red, as is to be expected from the common name used in the United States. The cheeks are yellow, which accounts for the alternative name of yellow-cheeked Amazon. The crown and nape are bluish

Blue-fronted Amazon, *Amazona aestiva aestiva.*

purple. Feathers of the lower nape and back are dark green and have dusky scalloping. Wing primaries are blue-black and green. The bend of the wing is red. The tail is green with a yellowish green band, as in many other Amazons. There is also a white eye ring on this Amazon.

Red-lored Amazons have been bred and hatched in the United States. Hym Prenner has owned Amazons for years in central Iowa, and his favorite is the red-lored Amazon. He claims he has never seen a mean red-lored. To set up the birds for breeding, he took a small wine barrel which was well sealed, made a 14-inch hole in one side and equipped the barrel with a perch. He put about one pound of peat in the bottom, then another two inches of wood shavings over the peat. He repeated this for each pair of red-lored Amazons.

His primary pair produced two eggs within a four-month period. Unfortunately, these eggs were infertile. It must be noted here that infertility in young first-time breeders is quite common. It seems to take Amazons a couple of nests before hatchability occurs. After three repeat tries, this pair of red-lored Amazons successfully incubated and raised three babies. In total, Mr. Prenner hatched 22 baby red-lored Amazons; I believe that this is still the record.

Our Pedro loved to hang on the shirt of our son Daren. Daren could also twirl Pedro around by the feet as if he were a ferris wheel. Pedro loved to say "Hello, Daren." We had a small black and white cat that loved to tease Pedro. Perhaps the cat expected Pedro to become a meal. At any rate, Pedro played until he was tired. When he took a healthy bite of the cat's tail, we knew playtime was over. This was a repetitive thing. It seemed that the cat loved to ask for trouble and a painful tail while Pedro enjoyed the entire procedure.

In addition to Pedro, we had another true pair of red-lored Amazons. They eventually went to nest and after three tries succeeded in hatching two chicks. Unfortunately, when the chicks were about six weeks of age the parents suddenly killed both of them. We were depressed, as we were comparatively new at the hard, most difficult game of breeding Amazons. We decided to experiment with feeding; on the next hatch we decided to increase the protein by utilizing meat. We fed a canned dog meat of good quality.

It was indeed a surprise to see the red-lored Amazons devour the meat. Their consumption of this dog food increased twofold after the chicks hatched. This time the chicks fledged well and were the most active and healthy young parrots I had seen.

DIADEMED AMAZON
Amazona autumnalis diadema

This is a rare, seldom imported Amazon, although in an era where over sixty private importers bring in thousands of parrots, a few come in as green-cheeks and Finsch's Amazons.

This bird is distinguished from Salvin's Amazon by only one feature: small red feathers cover the nostrils and the cere of this Amazon. I studied many bird skins at Peabody Museum at Yale University and at the Los Angeles County Museum and was able to differentiate Salvin's from diademeds; on each skin the only difference was the presence or absence of the red feathers over the nostrils. Salvin's Amazon does not have these tiny feathers.

To the best of my knowledge, I have never seen a living diademed Amazon. Even museum skins of this bird are rare. This subspecies is found only in northwestern Brazil, while its look-alike, Salvin's, is found in Colombia, Nicaragua, Costa Rica and Venezuela. It would be worth while to note just how rare this Amazon is in the wild. We do not know.

Opposite:
Close-up of an orange-winged's head. *Right:* a good view of the yellow at the bend of the wing on a blue-fronted. *Below:* a pair of blue-fronted Amazons.

LILACINE AMAZON
Amazona autumnalis lilacina

Here again is an Amazon that is constantly confused with another more popular bird, Finsch's Amazon, *Amazona finschi finschi*. This Amazon also has a red front with bright yellowish green cheeks, sometimes a very light yellow green. The red extends from the front over the eyes. In Finsch's Amazon there is no red over the eyes. The feathers of the crown of the lilacine are edged in lilac. The primary wing feathers are green, turning to blue at the tips; secondaries are green, becoming blue towards the tips. The base of the first five secondaries are red. The back is green, showing yellowish green at the tips. The bill is gray. Of all characteristics, however, the red streak over the eye, the lilac edges of the crown feathers and the yellow-green cheeks are uppermost in importance.

We do not own any lilacine Amazons, but a friend in Rhode Island owns one that is extremely tame. This bird is named Lilac and is a constant companion to a woolly monkey. The parrot is so attached to the monkey that when a human approaches the monkey, the parrot immediately goes into a spasm of terror. When the parrot is approached, the woolly monkey attacks. Consequently, the owner is in fear of handling either the parrot or the monkey.

Another aviculturist owns three true lilacine Amazons. All three are extremely tame, but their vocabulary is meager. Two of them are soft-ball-playing characters. They actually play ball by rolling the softball with their beaks from one to another.

The lilacine Amazon is not seen frequently in this country. Many Finsch's Amazons are seen, though, and too many Finsches are called lilacines.

SALVIN'S AMAZON
Amazona autumnalis salvini

Here is an Amazon that lacks the yellow that exists in the red-lored Amazon, *A. autumnalis autumnalis*. *A.a. salvini* has a red front and bright green cheeks and ear coverts. Too frequently, the Salvin's Amazon is called a green-cheeked Amazon. The green-cheeked, however, has a red front and crown in addition to the bright green cheek. Salvin's has a blue crown that extends to the nape of the neck. All other feathers of the back and the breast are dark green with an edge of duskiness.

Wings and tail are similar in color to those of the red-lored Amazon; both subspecies exhibit a white eye ring. This author has seen several Salvin's Amazons throughout the United States, yet few people realize they have them. Perhaps with education and practice, future Amazon lovers and breeders will learn to recognize this noisy but beautiful subspecies.

We have a pair of Salvin's Amazons that screech excessively, particularly when strangers appear in the vicinity of the aviaries. The male, correctly named Noisy, creates a perfect imitation of a guinea fowl. In attempting to trace the history of my pair, I discovered from the former owners that the birds came from an avicultural estate that specialized in peafowl and guinea fowl. This explained the peculiar guinea fowl uproar. Actually, the birds have proved to be exceptional watchdogs. For example, one evening, our aviaries were invaded by an unwelcome visitor, a raccoon. We heard a terrific racket created by our "guinea fowl" parrots. Upon investigation, a very nervous and retreating raccoon soon disappeared, hopefully never to appear again.

The female, named Noisier, simply screeches to ex-

Left: blue-fronted subspecies, *Amazona aestiva xanthopteryx.*

Right: black-billed Amazon, *Amazona agilis. Opposite:* white-fronted Amazon, *Amazona albifrons albifrons.*

tremes. She has a habit of laying one egg a year and sitting on this egg for about two days. Yet she protects the egg with a pugnacious attitude as if it has already hatched. Eventually, after weeks and weeks of guarding the egg very well, she disposes of it. We don't expect that this pair will ever reproduce. We call them our psycho pair of parrots.

We have friends in Maryland who have a pair of Salvin's Amazons. They argue that they have a pair of green-cheeked Amazons, although we know all the characteristics fit the classification of Salvin's. This pair is also extremely loud and noisy; they swear with a vocabulary of every four-letter word I have ever heard and some that I haven't. They will also bite the hand that feeds them. If ever there was a pair of spoiled parrots, that is the pair. Yet the owners love them immensely and exhibit their pride very frequently. No one knows where they picked up their strong language, but their enunciation is perfect. They thrive on beer, and their vocabulary—dirty as it is—increases with vulgarity and intensity, when they drink.

Comical and noisy as they are, Salvin's Amazon remains a poorly known, often misidentified subspecies.

YELLOW-SHOULDERED
AMAZON
Amazona barbadensis barbadensis

Rare and costly are good terms for the yellow-shouldered Amazon parrot. On the very few occasions when one can find a yellow-shoulder available it is indeed costly.

The front or forehead of the yellow-shouldered Amazon is white. This merges gradually into yellow about the crown. The area around the eyes is also yellow. The rear crown has a bluish tinge to the green feathers going into the nape. The feathers of the upper back and breast are dark

Salvin's Amazon, Amazona autumnalis salvini.

Amazona albifrons, encompassing three subspecies, is probably the most abundant Amazon in aviculture.

Escaped Amazons: Finsch's Amazon, *Amazona finschi* (top), and white-fronted Amazon, *Amazona albifrons*.

green edged with black. The abdomen feathers are not as distinctly edged in black.

In reviewing skins in various museums, I noted that vent or cloacal areas on all birds examined were blue. The shoulders as well as the thighs are also bright yellow. There is much yellow color in both these areas. Red is seen at the base of the tail, with yellow at the tips. Flight feathers are blue, black and green with a red speculum.

I have seen many skins as well as two living specimens at the Mayaguez zoo in Puerto Rico. This was a beautiful pair of birds having a great amount of yellow at the bend of the wing.

It amazes me that the Department of the Interior has listed several other more common birds as endangered yet pays little attention to this Amazon. We do not believe this Amazon to be extinct, but it is darn close! You may *never* see a living one. You will also have to visit many museums before you are able to study many skins. Hopefully somewhere in the world there is a self-sustaining group of yellow-shouldered Amazons.

ROTHSCHILD'S AMAZON
Amazona barbadensis rothschildi

Rothschild's Amazon is extremely rare, but we occasionally see a few in collections throughout the world.

There is much less yellow on the crown, bend of wing and thighs in Rothschild's than in the yellow-shouldered Amazon. Rothschild's does not have blue on the cheeks or hindcrown.

The yellow at the bend of the wing is a beautiful buttercup of brilliant yellow, with some red on some, but not all, individuals.

It was my fortunate experience to judge on more than one occasion some very strong groups of Amazons in which at least one Rothschild's was represented. Each bird was presented in unblemished condition, of good feather quality and steady on the bench. The color of these Amazons is superb. On one such occasion I came very close to selecting a Rothschild's as Best Amazon in a class of twenty. The particular specimen was a bit thin, having previously undergone a strenuous illness; it lacked some flesh on the upper breast.

Most recently I have noted splendid Rothschild's Amazons at the San Diego zoo and at the Tangowood aviaries of Linda Rubin of Brookline, Mass. These birds are in good feather. Perhaps there are others in collections over the country.

Needless to say, we hope breeders attempt to place these rare birds on breeding loan for the benefit of reproduction. We are entering an era in which aviculturists must begin to match breeding stock and attempt to raise progeny. If they don't, certain types of birds such as Rothschild's Amazon will disappear completely from both domestic stocks and the wild.

Even now there are several countries that prohibit the export of parrots and other birds. Periodically, we review reports that indicate another country has blocked the exportation of parrots. We fully expect that there will always be a few parrots coming into the States; we predict, however, that the rare ones will get rarer.

Owners of single Amazons should let it be known that they have a bird available for breeding, particularly if the bird is a rarity. We realize that many Amazons are good pets and extremely tame, but in my opinion there is nothing to the notion that a tame Amazon is not a good breeder; I consider it a myth. I have had more success with my tame Amazons and other parrots than with those thought to be wild and those so-called broncos (a bronco be-

The male (shown opposite page) white-fronted's wing is spread out so that the colors are displayed. This male bred with a female whose wing is shown on the opposite page.

Opposite:
This display of the female white-fronted's wing shows a much duller array of colors than the male's wing.

In 1978, Horst Müller successfully bred two white-fronted Amazons. *Right:* the male parent.

ing a parrot that would just as soon bite you as look at you). Fortunately, the Rothschild's Amazons I have seen were certainly not broncos.

RED-TAILED AMAZON
Amazona brasiliensis

Amazona brasiliensis is an extremely rare bird in both its native Brazil and in the hands of aviculturists.

The front of this Amazon is dark reddish pink; progressing to the crown, each feather is gradually more pinkish red. The nape becomes bluish green to green with black edging in each feather. The cheeks and throat as well as the lores are bluish pink, while ear coverts are less pinkish blue. The upper throat and thighs are light yellowish green. Upper and under tail coverts are yellowish green. The tail is unique in coloring in that the tips are yellow with a band of bright red leading to a base of green. The bend of the wing is red, with primary feathers of green ending with violet blue. Secondaries are also green, becoming violet blue. This is another very attractive Amazon. It is easily differentiated by the pinkish colors of the head and the red and yellow bands of the tail.

The red-tailed Amazon is virtually unknown at import stations and broker headquarters. In my travels to numerous zoos throughout the United States and the Caribbean I have seen no red-tailed Amazons, although I have seen a most attractive individual in a private home within a few miles of my own home. A fine bird-loving couple has not only this spectacular Amazon but also six other parrots—all quite rare. This fabulous red-tailed Amazon is tame and easily handled; he eats toast and coffee with his owner each morning, and he loves shrimp. He mimics his owners with clarity. He talks incessantly when boiled shrimp are available. He prefers boiled shrimp to sunflower seed and apples, bananas or crackers. When shrimp are not available, carrots become a fast favorite. "Crimson," as this Amazon is called, loves to chant "Let's go to a flea market." He also perfectly mimics the cuckoo clock. He does this so frequently and so perfectly that his owners never know the exact time if measured by the sound of the clock. When Bill, his owner, gets ready to eat breakfast, Crimson is always allowed out of his cage. He immediately flies to the table and partakes of some toast; he loves coffee with cream direct from his owner's cup.

I am constantly amazed at the number of rare parrots owned by this couple. Their collection began in the mid-1960's in New York City. All of their rare parrots were purchased from one pet store that advertised as specialists in rare and unusual birds and animals. This, of course, preceded the period of quarantined birds as well as the short era in which all birds were banned. It also followed the long period during which public health authorities banned all the importation of parrot-like birds because of psittacosis. The period in which our friend bought his birds (the late 1960's) brought in several rare Amazons at very reasonable prices.

It is indeed a thrill to see this rare Amazon in action, to see a rare Amazon in vivid color. If you haven't seen a red-tailed Amazon, look for one.

YELLOW-BILLED AMAZON
Amazona collaria

The yellow-billed Amazon, or Jamaican parrot, was also called the white-fronted Amazon in the nineteenth century.

The white-fronted youngster developed an abnormal foot; the reason for this malformation was not known.

Opposite
(Top): Müller's birds produced a clutch of two eggs. Unfortunately only one egg hatched. *Below:* Müller fed the youngster, here shown at two weeks of age, a vitamin supplement.

117

Today in Europe it is also called the red-throated Amazon.

This is an extremely rare Amazon, seldom seen in the United States before 1979, although a few birds were seen in private collections. I know of only three in New York and four in separate collections in Florida prior to the entrance of several hundred birds through various import quarantine centers in 1979.

W.T. Greene, famous avicultural author of the 1880's, indicated that the yellow-billed Amazon was decreasing in numbers very rapidly in the early 1880's. This bird was extremely destructive to oranges in Jamaica, so even as far back as 1885 people were talking about its possible extinction.

This is a small Amazon. The front and lores are white; this white extends around the eye and to the ear coverts. Ear coverts are bluish green. The entire throat area is a pinkish red. This color extends around the edges of the nape. The crown is bluish, extending to green with black edges clear to the nape and including the nape. There is pink and yellow at the base of the tail; yellow is distinct at the tips of the tail feathers. Wing primaries are dark blue; secondaries are lighter. The bill is light yellow. General body color is green. Feathers of the breast and lower abdomen do not have the black edging seen in most other Amazons.

The yellow-billed Amazon will nest in hollow trees, particularly breadfruit and acacia trees. Natives will search for hollows in trees and watch for activity. If they see adult parrots they generally scale the tree and remove the baby birds. Generally each nest will contain three babies. The natives will feed the young by chewing bananas, then allowing the young birds to eat the bananas from their mouths. As they grow up the birds are given other foods such as boiled rice and baked roots which are similar to yams and white sweet potatoes.

On a trip to Jamaica in 1972, I witnessed a few yellow-billed Amazons for sale in the farmers' markets, but before 1979 one seldom saw this Amazon advertised for sale in the United States. It is quite probable that the rush of yellow-billed Amazons into the United States in 1979 will be the last. It appears that this Amazon is becoming rarer.

People who own them consider them to be good talkers and very affectionate pets. Their beauty excels. It would be worthwhile to see a breeding program started to maintain this Amazon's numbers above the threateningly low level state that now exists.

In Jamaica, the yellow-billed Amazon frequents the mountain areas. They travel to the orange orchards, as this is their favorite fruit. They open up the oranges, sucking up most of the juices. When filled, they fly back to their mountain retreat. Jamaica is known for the John Crow Mountains and the Blue Mountains; the yellow-billed Amazon seems to prefer the John Crow Mountains, although there are a few on the Blue Mountains.

BLUE-CHEEKED AMAZON
Amazona dufresniana dufresniana

A most attractive Amazon, but one that is seldom seen, is the blue-cheeked. I have seen a few in zoos and private collections, but one literally never sees them on import listings and broker price lists.

The cheeks of this Amazon are dark blue extending to the throat and progressing to a bluish green at the lower throat. The breast is bluish. The front is yellowish orange and the crown is yellowish green. General plumage is dark green, although the outer tail feathers are dark blue. Primaries of the wing are yellow and secondaries are dark blue.

It was my pleasure to travel to the interior, elevated coun-

The wings of this young white-fronted Amazon did not have the same rate of development.

Opposite
(Top): The eyes of the youngster at two weeks of age are barely open. *Below:* at four weeks, the eyes are fully opened and the bird appears quite alert.

121

try of Guyana. This trip was made with two other veterinarians in search of the vampire bat. During this sojourn I was extremely fortunate to view a few blue-cheeked Amazons. They seem to enjoy higher elevations and do not dwell in hot, arid areas. We did not see very many blue-cheeks, but it was a great thrill to see the few flying in the area. I must concur with other writers who have indicated that the blue-cheeked Amazon, also called Dufresne's Amazon is extremely rare, both in its native land and in captivity.

There has been a very docile and delightful blue-cheeked Amazon exhibited at the Capron Park Zoo in Attleboro, Massachusetts for several years. This bird typifies the blue-cheeked Amazon. It does, however, seem to pair up with a plain-colored Amazon, even though several parrots, mostly Amazons, are exhibited together.

One long-time friend and aviculturist has owned a blue-cheeked Amazon for twenty years. This blue-cheeked has patterned the voice of Harry's wife to perfection. "Harry, Harry," the blue-cheeked enunciates perfectly. This always confused Harry since it is a perfect copy of Harry's wife. Many times Harry answers the bird, thinking his wife had called him. It is almost scary to him, particularly when his wife is away. The bird also loves to show off in front of company. He enjoys saying, "Give me a beer. Give me a big beer. Give me a great big beer." Although I reiterate that as a group the double yellow-head, the yellow-naped and the Panama are the better talkers, I can truthfully say that this individual blue-cheeked Amazon, aptly named "Speaker," is the best clearest-talking parrot I have ever heard.

Truly, one can appreciate the blue-cheeked Amazon, not only for its beauty, its rarity and its docile character, but also for its evidence as a talker.

RED-CAPPED AMAZON
Amazona dufresniana rhodocorytha

Few people realize the closeness of the red-capped Amazon and the blue-cheeked Amazon, perhaps because of the divergence of common names; the scientific names of the birds of course point out the close relationship between them.

There is much less blue on the cheeks of the red-capped Amazon. In addition, the blue that does occur is a much lighter sky blue. The front is scarlet, extending to the forecrown. Here each succeeding feather of the crown is green with red edging. Males have a yellow tinge on each feather of the scarlet front; females have much less yellow evident. Feathers of the hindcrown are purplish red edged with bluish black. The lores are yellow orange.

The tail is green tipped with yellow; lateral feathers of the tail are heavily marked with red. Secondaries of the wing are red, purple and blue. General body plumage is lighter green than in the blue-cheeked.

This subspecies, very attractive in flight, is readily available in the wilds of Surinam, but it is seldom imported. I have seen only a very few of these Amazons in the coastal area of Surinam.

My viewing of the red-capped Amazon in captivity has been rare. Only two aviaries, to my knowledge, house one or more red-capped Amazons. One extremely advanced aviculturist has two pair, one of which is copulating and preparing to nest constantly. The female of the other pair has laid two infertile eggs. The owner's formula for feeding preconditioned breeding Amazons is of interest. He mixes in three equal parts dry dog chow, boiled white rice and safflower seed. To this, which has a thick, moist consistency, is added about two pounds of raisins. The sum total is

124

At ten weeks of age, the young white-fronted shows his "true colors."

Opposite:
(Top): A hint of red lores to come can be seen in the six-week-old youngster. *Below:* by eight weeks, the red, white and green feathers in the head region have developed.

about twenty pounds. He then freezes this mixture in individual cartons for feeding when needed. He ensures that each frozen carton is thoroughly thawed and warmed before feeding. His parrots love it and seem to do well on it. Other species are breeding successfully on this mixture.

With luck, his red-capped Amazons will thrive and reproduce well on this diet, about which it is worthy to note the absence of sunflower seeds, the fattening food.

MEALY AMAZON
Amazona farinosa farinosa

Too many aviculturists and too many bird show judges do not know the color differences between the subspecies of this *Amazona farinosa*. Actually, the differentiating points among the four subspecies (mealy Amazon, *A. farinosa farinosa;* plain-colored Amazon, *A.f. inornata;* blue-crowned Amazon, *A.f. guatemalae;* green-headed Amazon, *A.f. virenticeps*) are all on the head. The true mealy Amazon must have some yellow feathers on either the front or the crown or both. The plain-colored has a mauve or grayish blue series of feathers on the crown. The blue-crowned has cobalt blue or bright blue feathering on the crown. As the name implies, the green-headed has bright dark green feathers on the entire head.

The true mealy Amazon is frequently imported into the United States. I know of several aviculturists and pet owners who have specimens. My good friends John and Irene Hughes of Nashua, New Hampshire have a positively fine mealy Amazon. They have repeatedly made the statement that this is one of the most docile and quiet parrots they have ever owned. Yet I have a mealy that, although very docile, is also extremely noisy.

One of my fortunate Amazon parrot breeding successes was the hatching and raising of two baby mealy Amazons. The male mealy parent was seven years of age; the female was nine years. They had been together in a 6'x6'x6' pen for four years with no sign of going into the garbage can nest, but one June day I noticed that the pair had started to spend more and more time in the nest box. By late June the female remained in the garbage nest box. We dared not peek in, so we waited patiently for an opportune time. One day in July we decided to look; there were two naked babies. The thrill was present and still is whenever we see newly hatched parrots.

Through constant feeding of numerous products, my wife Helen successfully persuaded the parents to fully care for both babies to full maturity. Helen fed no less than the following: bread and milk daily, cheese, apples, safflower seed, honey and mashed bananas, sunflower seed and grapes as well as dog food and monkey chow.

The babies fledged in two months; they were easily handled and became very good pets. They are thriving well today.

The mealy Amazon has a variable number of yellow feathers on the front or crown or on both front and crown. Feathers of the front, crown and nape that are not yellow are green edged in black. In the wing the primary feathers are black with blue and green. Secondaries have red in addition to black, blue and green. The tail is dark green with yellow tips. There is red at the bend of the wing.

The skins I have studied show, in contrast to skins of plain-colored Amazons, that the nominate subspecies in general is smaller than the plain-colored. I have measured some mealy Amazons at seventeen inches and at least two plain-colored Amazons at a record nineteen inches. I would not hesitate to say that the plain-colored Amazon is the second largest of all the Amazons, exceeded only by the great and grand imperial Amazon.

The male parent's head can be compared to his male offspring's head shown at the top of the facing page.

Opposite:
The parent white-fronteds are shown together with their offspring (far right). Note the youngster's malformed foot.

BLUE-CROWNED AMAZON
Amazona farinosa guatemalae

Perhaps the reason I enjoy the blue-crowned Amazon so greatly is that it resembles the plain-colored, which has been so close to our family for so many years. The blue-crowned Amazon is an excellent talker. Individual birds are noisy at times, but they can remain very quiet for long periods of time. I know of several blue-crowns in many collections. Many of these birds are excellent talkers, and some have extensive vocabularies.

Many blue-crowned Amazons have been imported into the United States in the latter part of the 1970's. Most brokers and importers have had them for sale.

One problem that must be encountered by the aviculturist or pet buyer involves the subspecies you receive regardless of what you order. Too many brokers and importers cannot differentiate among the subspecies. Even if they can, many times they could care less about which birds they will ship to you.

One close friend purchased two plain-colored Amazons by phone to be shipped a long distance. Both were very nice birds, but only one was a plain-colored; the other was a true mealy. Another friend definitely wanted two blue-crowned Amazons, since he preferred their color and their actions. He purchased direct from an importer, one whose prices are considerably lower than the normal, and two true mealies, two *Amazona farinosa farinosa,* duly arrived. Both birds had numerous yellow feathers on their crown, which should have been an immediate tip-off as to their true taxonomic status, but the shipper either didn't know or didn't care. That's one of the dangers of buying birds by mail. It is almost impossible to secure proper replacements when one is dealing with many subspecies of a species. Personally, I prefer purchasing direct from a breeder. However, occa-

130

sionally an importer or broker may be the only source. Therefore I realize that importers and brokers are very necessary.

The blue-crowned Amazon differs from the other members of the species in that the crown and hindcrown are bright blue. The front and nape are green, with black edging on each feather. The bend of the wing is red. Each primary wing feather is black, blue and green. Secondaries are black, blue, green and red. The tail is green, turning yellowish green at the tips. General body color is the typical dark Amazon parrot green.

PLAIN-COLORED AMAZON
Amazona farinosa inornata

One of my favorites of the entire Amazon group is the large plain-colored Amazon. We have a pair of these colorful and highly intelligent birds. In our opinion, these birds are not "plain"—but I guess it all depends on which colors you may like.

Sam is our favorite; she talks, cries, barks and whistles in many ways. She is a large bird, eighteen inches long. She was originally thought to be a male, as her name implies. She loves to nibble on whole lemons, eventually devouring the entire lemon. Her next favorite is the apple; however, she is a fruit lover, enjoying all varieties. Both of our plain-colored Amazons love not only all fruits but also peanuts and peanut butter. They also particularly relish wheat germ. They also relish fun foods such as chocolate candy and bubblegum balls. I believe that such oddball foods aren't harmful as long as they're strictly limited. What a comic Sam becomes when she attempts to chew a bubble-gum ball. The manipulation of her mouth invariably

Smaller than most Amazons, the orange-winged, *Amazona amazonica,* is also characterized by light blue front and lores (left) and a clear orange color in the wings and tail (below).

A young orange-winged Amazon.

creates the impression of the true clown Sam really is.

Sam delights in riding on the shoulder of our son. She is as kind and passive a bird as we have seen in the many years we have been associated with Amazons. She enjoys teasing other parrots as well as certain members of the dog family. She loves to call the names of our Bulldogs.

The bill of the plain-colored Amazon is horn-gray in color, sometimes shading to ivory at the base. Legs and feet are gray. The front or forehead is made up of light green feathers. The crown appears to be a definite dull bluish gray, but actually each feather is gray at the base for a quarter of each feather, then dull green for the next half of the feather, with the final quarter being a dull bluish gray. The nape appears brighter, each feather being an apple green bordered by a fine gray scalloped edge. The back feathers are distinctly grayish green, appearing very dull. This carries through to the outer wing coverts.

Primary wing feathers are green at the base; they fade into black, giving the open wing a definite black appearance. Approximately five feathers over towards the secondaries, one-half of each primary feather starts to show bright blue; each succeeding feather exhibits more blue as the black tends to diminish. The secondaries appear blue, fading to blue and green and eventually green alone. The immediate coverts are beautiful blue and red; also green and red feathers occur. The tail of the plain-colored Amazon is bright green at the base of each feather; it brightens to a distinct light greenish yellow. This is an exquisite bird—plain in color, but exquisite.

One other characteristic involves the white eye ring around a large eye. This ring is distinctive. The eye is alert, indicative of an Amazon with much mischief and love.

This species is found mainly in Panama, western Colombia and extreme western Venezuela.

The major difference between the plain-colored Amazon and the mealy Amazon is the complete lack of yellow on or

A plain-colored Amazon, *Amazona farinosa inornata*—this is Sam, one of the author's show winners.

Right: Two Panama Amazons, *Amazona ochrocephala panamensis.* One is the blue mutation. *Below:* The Grand Cayman Amazon, *Amazona leucocephala caymanensis,* though extremely rare, is currently being bred by a few aviculturists in the U.S.A.

about the head; there should be no yellow on the plain-colored Amazon. This writer strongly believes that the plain-colored Amazon is the strongest, most reliable sub-species of *Amazona farinosa*. The plain-colored Amazons I have seen have consistently been the most intelligent birds of the species.

They love to nest in the hollow sections of the highest trees in the deepest of jungles. They seldom lay over two eggs. These eggs are extremely large in size, almost the size of a small bantam egg. They are white in color. The incubation period varies from 28 to 30 days. In eight to twelve weeks the fledglings leave the nest, generally for good.

True plain-colored Amazons are comparatively rare; in my travels to zoos and aviaries around the world, I have seen only half a dozen other plain-colored Amazons besides my own.

Sam and Sally (Sally is a male), as previously mentioned, are active participants in talking sessions as well as spray bathing sessions. They love to be sprayed with warm water in a fine, fine spray. Sam will spread her wings and fluff her feathers with joy. She will take this for hours if we let her endure it for that long a period. When stopped, she will continue to display her extended wings. Meanwhile, Sally will enjoy his display in a similar manner.

I'll say again that the plain-colored Amazon is one of the very large Amazons. It is larger than the true mealy and the blue-crowned Amazon by at least an inch. We have measured several Amazons; in general, most of the plain-coloreds are larger.

Some authors and taxonomists claim that another subspecies of *A. farinosa* can be differentiated from *A.f. inornate;* they call this subspecies *A.f. chapmani.* I do not recognize this subspecies, as there are not even minor differentiating characteristics between individual specimens regardless of geographic origin.

GREEN-HEADED AMAZON
Amazona farinosa virenticeps

Of the four subspecies of *Amazona farinosa*, the green-headed Amazon is the least popular, least frequently imported and least frequently owned by pet owners and aviculturists. Because of its solid green color, few people select this Amazon, despite its availability from Central America.

I do know of several green-headed Amazons in the hands of pet owners and aviculturists. They are as fine and docile Amazons as the mealy and the plain-colored. To the best of my knowledge, no green-headed Amazons have been hatched and successfully raised in the United States.

The entire head is green; occasionally there is a slight blue tinge on the crown. The nape and general body color is dark Amazon parrot green. The area of the upper breast and abdomen is yellowish green. The bend of the wing is also green. Wing primaries are green, blue and black; secondaries are red, black, blue and green. Like the tails of other *A. farinosa* subspecies the tail is green with yellow green tips.

One parrot-owning couple in North Dakota has only one parrot, and this parrot is a green-headed Amazon. This couple wouldn't part with "Greenie" for a million bucks. This is the nicest, friendliest, most comforting, talkingest parrot they have ever seen. They bought "Greenie" eighteen years ago in a Cleveland, Ohio bird shop. According to them, this is the best buy they ever made.

Their feeding practices are different. "Greenie" eats only the foods eaten by the family. His favorites include mashed potatoes, cooked sweet potatoes (preferably baked), fried chicken, hamburger patties, green beans and corn on the cob. He loves to drink hot chocolate—and the small marshmallows floating on the hot chocolate are his biggest treat.

This reminds me of my plain-colored Amazon, Sam, with

It is clear to see why the red-lored Amazon is also called the yellow-cheeked Amazon.

Opposite:
The red lores of *A. autumnalis* are obvious on this impressively posed bird. The dark bill characterizes *lilacina;* the overall yellow cast, however, is an artifact of the photograph.

whom we have had an eighteen-year association. Just look at the longevity of both of these birds. In both cases, our Amazons are on the way to a long association with their families.

BODIN'S AMAZON
Amazona festiva bodini

We discuss the rarity of the festive Amazon; Bodin's Amazon is even rarer, both in captivity and the wild. It occurs only in southwestern Venezuela and northwestern Guyana in the wild, so it is seldom imported. I know of only one Bodin's Amazon in captivity, although it is surprising where one may find certain birds. On a recent visit to a local cagebird association member's home, we were pleasantly surprised to see a gigantic and marvelous great black palm cockatoo as well as a splendid Bodin's Amazon. The owners had owned these birds for ten years or more. This was literally in my back yard.

Bodin's Amazon differs from the festive Amazon by having a lighter red front which extends into the crown. The remainder of the crown is green, with more blue throughout. The nape is green, with blacker edges than in the festive. The cheeks are blue. The throat and abdomen are lighter green. The rump is scarlet red. Immatures lack the red rump until the first molt.

Having seen only one Bodin's Amazon, I find it difficult to make a statement on the entire subspecies, but the one Bodin's Amazon with which I'm familiar is one of the mildest-mannered parrots I have ever seen. His owner states that this bird has never once nipped him or scratched him. The Amazon speaks a few choice words, particularly Hello and Goodbye.

Perhaps the most interesting aspect to me was that the

owner had been given the correct identification when he obtained the bird. Historically, through the decades of parrot history, most Bodin's Amazons are incorrectly labeled as festive Amazons. In reviewing the listings of importations into the United States in 1977, there were no entries for either *Amazona festiva festiva* or *Amazona festiva bodini.*

FESTIVE AMAZON
Amazona festiva festiva

It is unfortunate that this Amazon is so extremely rare in captivity. Those few I have seen have been most delightful in disposition and character.

Here is a bird that is basically dark green. A narrow frontal band of dark red, in contrast to the dark gray bill, is unique. The remaining front and crown are green with a bluish tinge. The cheeks are green; each feather of the nape and throat is green, with some black edging. Yellow edging is seen on green wing coverts. The most typical color characteristic is the bright scarlet red rump. There is no red at the bend of the wing; there also is no red speculum.

The festive Amazon ranks high as a bird with much talent not only as a talker but also as a friendly, amicable character. I know of one very tame and docile festive Amazon that was housed in an eastern zoo. The bird liked everybody except the zoo's curator. For some reason she hated the curator to such an extent that she screeched and attempted to bite him, particularly when visitors were around. The curator once told me, though, that she would allow him to pick her up when no one was around.

Another festive Amazon at a wild animal park in the east was also a very tame and docile bird. I tried in vain to buy this bird. Eventually, the park owners shipped it to Arizona. It arrived in Phoenix in dreadful heat, and the bird soon

Close-up of a yellow-billed Amazon, *Amazona collaria*.

became comatose; eventually it died. What a shame!—this bird is extremely rare in this country.

Although the festive Amazon is rare in the United States, we are told that it is still fairly common in Ecuador and Peru. We believe that because its general appearance is comparatively dull, the collectors and exporters pay little attention to this Amazon. It is noteworthy that the rump is not evident on general viewing. One has to watch the festive fly away to witness the scarlet rump.

We know of another fabulous talker in Ohio, classified correctly as a festive Amazon, that is a cheese lover. This festive will do anything for a piece of cheese. He begs by saying, "Cheese, Cheese." He will jump up and down, then take a somersault, all for a piece of cheese. He then devours the cheese as if he will never get another piece. This is indeed a festive Amazon with much personality. Our Ohio friend says that the bird lives up to its common name. He loves parties and literally has to be put away during some dinner parties, as his noise drowns out the dinner guests. Frequently, however, the dinner guests request him back to vocalize later in the evening. I was a dinner guest at this home, hoping that I would be fortunate enough to enjoy the antics of this bird, so aptly named "Festival." Typically, the owner retrieved the bird after dinner. Upon offering a piece of cheese to Festival, the owner sat back to watch the antics along with the guests. Every morsel of cheese was devoured—it was like watching a glutton devouring his first meal in a month. During the entire eating episode, Festival kept repeating the words "Cheese, Cheese." Such a joker!

It is true that cheese is an excellent food for parrots. As mentioned elsewhere in this text, cheese (accompanied, of course, by other nutritious foods) is a necessity for raising good strong babies.

I known of no successful breedings of the festive Amazon.

FINSCH'S AMAZON
Amazona finschi finschi

Here is another Amazon that is plentiful in the United States. This bird has a dark reddish maroon front and lores. The crown and feathers of the neck as well as down the lateral edges of the nape are lilac in color. The actual green feathers of the nape are edged in lilac also (that is why this Amazon is known to some as the lilac-crowned Amazon.) The chin and breast feathers are green edged in black.

Primary wing feathers are violet blue, becoming a dark green at the base. As in other closely related species, the first five secondary wing feathers are based in red. Other secondaries are green, becoming blue towards the tips, Wing coverts are dark green. The tail is green with yellowish green tips.

The most distinguishing characteristic that differentiates Finsch's Amazon from Salvin's (*A. autumnalis salvini*) and the lilacine Amazon (*A. autumnalis lilacina*) is the cheek color. The cheeks of Finsch's Amazon are dull green, in contrast to a bright green in Salvin's and a yellowish green in the lilacine. Also note that a red line extends over the eye in the lilacine; this line is not present in Finsch's Amazon.

Another attractive and contrasting characteristic in Finsch's Amazon involves the lovely lilac purple color of the crown, which encircles both cheeks. A Finsch's Amazon in good color and condition can be a most attractive and fascinating bird.

Perhaps the most beautiful Finsch's Amazon I have seen is exhibited at Busch Gardens in Los Angeles, California. This particular bird was in such superb condition and color that I could see it winning high honors in any bird show.

Literally thousands of Finsch's Amazons have been imported into the United States since 1973. They are common and popular; consequently, one can purchase a

Left: a close-up of the head of a red-lored Amazon. *Below:* two green-cheeked Amazons.

Yellow extending down onto the neck and the breast characterizes the Tres Marias Amazon, *Amazona ochrocephala tresmariae.* The extensive yellow, plus the red, makes this form one of the most colorful amazons.

Finsch's Amazon for less than one hundred dollars. I have known at least a half dozen aviculturists who have successfully bred this subspecies.

One Ohio aviculturist stated that his pair was six years old when the female laid two eggs in a hollow log nest area. On the 27th day, upon inspecting the nesting hole, he discovered that one chick had hatched. The other egg had a dead chick in the shell. The living chick was left with the parents; it fledged and left the nest at three and a half months of age.

An aviculturist in Louisiana wrote to me stating that his birds were at least four years old when they went to nest in a converted garbage can. He used cedar shavings and black dirt in the base of the can. The hen laid two eggs; both hatched in 28 days. (The eggs were laid two days apart and hatched two days apart.) These chicks left the nest at four months and one week, fledging at this time.

A third aviculturist, this one in Massachusetts, owns a pair of Finsch's Amazons that he purchased prior to the large Newcastle outbreak in California which occurred in the early 1970's. He bought his birds in 1967. When these birds were nine years old they attempted to nest on the floor of a normal bird cage. The owner placed some cloth rags under the one egg already laid. Surprisingly, the female incubated the egg for 26 days; more surprisingly the chick hatched and the parents cared for the baby extremely well. It fledged in fifteen weeks and was cracking seed and eating alone by sixteen weeks.

The variables in these cases are interesting. Success was achieved using three contrasting types of nest boxes. (Actually, one used no nest at all.) I have doubted whether I would ever see success in the bottom of a cage.

The length of incubation of the various Amazon parrot species and subspecies has always intrigued me. The incubation time for *A.f. finschi* tends to vary from 26 to 28 days. Could environment and weather conditions cause this variability? I believe so. Could the female's activity on and off the eggs allow for a difference in hatching times? I believe this is also true.

Finally, it is apparent that fledging is the most variable aspect of production of young Finsch's Amazons. I believe that different parents feed better than others; perhaps some parents speed along the activity of reaching fledgling age by their keen interest in feeding the babies. Also, one aviculturist may be a better feeder than the next; this would affect the way the parents feed the young. Hand-reared young always seem to fledge slower than parent-fed babies. My belief has been founded on experience both ways. My preference is to let the parents feed the young if they will complete the chore. Of course, there are times that bird parents refuse to feed the young; then the human must take over.

Finally, there has to be a difference in fledging of young when there is a difference in number of young in the nest. One single baby should grow and fledge faster than a nest of two fledglings.

Finsch's Amazons will undoubtedly be bred in greater numbers through the next few years. Perhaps we will then learn much more about the variables mentioned.

WOOD'S LILAC-CROWNED AMAZON
Amazona finschi woodi

Wood's lilac-crowned Amazon could be described as a Finsch's Amazon with a darker green plumage of somewhat duller appearance. This subspecies also has a much narrower band of red at the front in comparison to Finsch's

Right: the green-cheeked Amazon (top) shares a flight with an unusual Amazon. On the lower bird, the head markings (as distinct from coloration) and the dark bill indicate the species *festiva*, and the coloration points to the subspecies *bodini*. However, this bird lacks the red rump of *festiva*, so it may be A. *dufresniana rhodocorytha*. *Below:* Lilacine Amazon, *A. autumnalis lilacina.*

Salvin's Amazon, *Amazona autumnalis salvini* (right), is often confused with the green-cheeked Amazon, *A. viridigenalis* (below).

153

Amazon. It is found only in the states of Chihuahua and Sonora in Mexico. It is believed that about ten per cent of all Finsch's Amazon importations are actually Wood's lilac-crowned Amazons.

A review of skins at Yale University and at the Los Angeles Museum revealed that the 10% figure fits bird skins on record—90% of the skins examined were true Finsch's Amazons, with the rest being Wood's lilac-crowned Amazons. The *A.f. woodi* skins almost all had narrower, darker red fronts and a much darker green general plumage.

Since most persons cannot differentiate *Amazona finschi woodi* from *Amazona finschi finschi,* there are apparently no disagreements that can develop when one is purchased at a pet shop or aviary.

One interesting incident occurred at a pet shop that handles many birds. This pet shop had two Finsch's Amazons and advertised them as such. On close inspection, though, it turned out that one was a Wood's. A young couple showed immense interest in purchasing a Finsch Amazon. It took them no longer than one minute to select the *Amazona f. finschi;* they were overheard saying that the other one was too dark in color. This indeed sums up Wood's lilac-crowned Amazon.

ST. VINCENT AMAZON
Amazona guildingi

A rare and endangered Amazon originating on a tiny island of the Lesser Antilles, the St. Vincent Amazon, one of the largest birds in the genus, was named for the island on which it lives. It is as beautiful as it is different in color from all other Amazons.

Here is a case where environment played a great part in the dwindling of a species. In the late 1800's, a terrific hurricane literally wiped out the St. Vincent Amazon. Hundreds were killed, according to island records. Then in 1902 a terrible volcanic eruption not only destroyed many more St. Vincent Amazons but the rest of the Carib population as well.

The Caribs were the original natives of the island as well as other islands of the Antilles. The island of St. Vincent lies at the lower end of the Caribbean chain. It is a small green island only eighteen miles long and eleven miles wide. An old impenetrable range of volcanic mountains runs through the island like a spine down its whole length of eighteen miles. The great crater of Soufriere, which has a crater lake in the center, rises to 4000 feet. There are many rivers on the island, mostly on the western side. On the east the land slopes gently to the coast. This 133-square mile island has fifteen thousand acres of land set aside as forest reserves. Hopefully, the slow-reproducing St. Vincent Amazon will make a gradual comeback, although the situation looks quite hopeless.

During the short period of time we were in Kingstown, which lies on the southwest coast below the foothills of Mt. St. Andrew, we spoke to several natives concerning the St. Vincent Amazon. One native indicated that we might see an occasional parrot on the jaunt between Kingston and Georgetown. We tried; we looked intently, but with no luck.

We also visited the botanical gardens where we saw a talipot palm tree in bloom (it blooms only once in its life span of seventy or so years), as well as an offshoot of the original breadfruit tree planted by Captain Bligh of H.M.S. *Bounty* fame. Yet we saw no St. Vincent Amazons. I was taken along two rivers into a forest area without seeing a St. Vincent Amazon. (A census taken in early 1978 revealed no more than five hundred St. Vincent Amazons on the

Rothschild's Amazon, *Amazona barbadensis rothschildi.*

Opposite:
(Top): Though it is not yet on the endangered list, the yellow-shouldered Amazon, *Amazona barbadensis barbadensis,* is an extremely rare bird, and it may be close to extinction. *Below:* note the red and yellow at the bend of the wing on this Rothschild's Amazon.

157

island.) I did manage to see one tame St. Vincent Amazon kept by a native of the island. It was a large, beautiful bird with good talking ability. The owner had maintained the bird for several years. It amazed me to view the diet of that bird. He was fed only rice, bananas and coconuts.

In studying St. Vincent Amazon skins at Peabody Museum, Yale University, I noted that the front and forecrown are white; lores are white turning to yellow; cheeks and throat are orange extending to the ear coverts. Wing speculum and coverts are bright orange. The hindcrown and upper nape are orange. There is an irregular area of blue over the ear coverts. Lower nape feathers are bluish bronze with a green tinge. This extends down the back. Abdomen and underpart feathers are brownish bronze. Primaries are black, with green edging ending in violet blue. Secondaries are violet blue with orange bases and centers of green; inner secondaries are dark green, becoming blue with orange bases. Secondary coverts are orange bronze. Tips of the tail are yellow; the bases are orange. The bulk of the tail in the center is bluish purple.

It appears that juveniles are greenish bronze, gradually turning more bluish violet and orange with age. There is still much debate on the subject.

There are a few St. Vincent Amazons in zoos in the United States. We know of one pair of St. Vincent Amazons in an aviary; the birds are close to thirty years of age, yet they have never produced young. We would hope that those in possession of breeding pairs of St. Vincent Amazons pursue the activity of breeding to save this rare and beautiful species. Those with single specimens should attempt to make arrangements with others in the same plight so that breeding possibilities can occur.

St. Vincent governmental authorities must concentrate on protection by tough regulations and good education. Natives must be persuaded not to eat parrots. There must be plenty of chicken available.

IMPERIAL AMAZON
Amazona imperialis

While on the island of Dominica I attempted to study the habitat preferences of the imperial Amazon in relation to those of the red-necked Amazon. It was noticeable that the red-necked enjoyed the lower forested areas along the rivers, whereas the imperial enjoyed the mountainous areas. It was also evident that the imperial was a good deal rarer than the red-necked. Native Dominicans told me that the mountainous forests are extremely entangled with jungle underbrush and high cliffs; that the imperial is seldom seen results from the difficulty humans have in maneuvering through this country.

A Dominican who made occasional trips to the Mosquito Mountains as a guide indicated that he frequently saw two or three imperial Amazons. Since I was in the Portsmouth area, I urged him to take me to the mountainous area, for I had never seen an imperial. Our Dominican guide stated that Mosquito Mountain was much too difficult to reach from Portsmouth but that we could go along the Picard River to Morne Turner. He was sure that the imperial lived in this mountain range. Between Morne Turner and Mosquito Mountain is a place called Morne Diablotins; he knew that this area, as well as Mount Macaque, were the stronghold areas of the grand imperial Amazon.

Our trip along the Picard River was exciting as any dream I had ever had. The thought that perhaps I would soon see the tremendous imperial brought anxious moments. As we progressed slowly in a most difficult jungle area with terrain unprecedented for me, we heard what we thought was a call of the imperial Amazon. During this entire rough journey we finally saw one pair of imperials. They were perched high in a fruit tree which I still

Two young yellow-billed Amazons, *Amazona collaria*. The slight rose color at the throat will deepen to pinkish red as the birds mature.

Opposite: A second view of the Amazon shown on page 152. Once again, the characters of *festiva bodini* are apparent. Further, the tail suggests *A. festiva,* since, though some feathers are missing, the remaining ones lack the red areas found in *A. dufresniana.* Mention of green-rumped birds with these characters has occurred in the literature, under the name *"chloronota,"* and assigned to *A. festiva.* Because of the rarity of such specimens, it remains uncertain whether they should be recognized as a separate subspecies of *A. festiva.* Other evidence suggests they may be hybrids of *A. festiva bodini* and *A. dufresniana dufresniana.*

cannot identify. Both were actively eating fruit which looked like immature apricots. When picked up and examined they were noted to be mostly hard seed with green pulp surrounding the seed.

The birds were exquisite in color but appeared very shy. We could not approach too closely. Consequently, I would not be able to describe the imperial from that brief viewing time. On this entire long excursion we didn't see another imperial, although we saw many other unusual and beautiful birds, including a couple of red-necked Amazons.

Back in the United States at Yale University, I was able to study some imperial skins. The entire head, neck, cheeks, throat, breast and abdomen are a dark bluish violet, each feather edged in black. The feathers of the back and flank are green with blue edgings. The tail is brownish green with green tips. There is red at the bend of the wing. Primary feathers of the wing are violet blue with green bases and brownish tips. Wing coverts are green. Secondaries are green ending with violet blue tips.

The imperial Amazon is extremely large, actually the largest of all the Amazons. Those skins I did study were 20 inches in length, which far exceeds the length of all other Amazons. This bird is truly well named. Not the rarest of Amazons, but still very rare, the imperial is not to be seen in aviaries or very many zoos to my knowledge. It is one of those rare and beautiful parrots that we can only hope to see, and if we are fortunate, we'll get a glimpse.

BAHAMAN AMAZON
Amazona leucocephala bahamensis

The largest and most brilliantly colored subspecies of *Amazona leucocephala* is the Bahaman Amazon. The white of the forehead and crown is more extensive than in any other of the five subspecies. It sometimes extends to the beginning of the nape of the neck. This white also extends to the lores and below the eyes to the upper cheek areas.

The rose color seems brighter and more colorful than any other rose I have ever seen. Often the maroon on the abdomen is absent or only partially visible. There is less red on the base areas of the tail feathers.

The only recent sightings of the Bahaman Amazon have occurred on Great Inagua Island of the Bahamas and Great Abaco Island of the Bahamas. We understand that less than six hundred Bahaman Amazons exist today, and conservationists are greatly concerned over the threatened population of these Amazons. We urge all breeders of Amazons to attempt to breed with selectivity and good hard work. The most severe problem, however, today is the fact that this bird is now protected on its native island, so breeders can't obtain individuals for breeding. If hunters and others continue to harm the Bahaman Amazon, then it is in the gravest danger. Only through selective breeding by aviculturists will rare species like this be saved. An example that remains high with me is the story of the most endangered parakeet, the turquoisine from Australia. This bird is just about extinct in its native habitat. However, dedicated aviculturists of the United States, Great Britain and other countries have bred this darling bird into domestication so well that the bird is now quite common in aviculture. Another example is the nene goose from Hawaii. It was nearly extinct in its native Hawaii, but through the dedicated efforts of aviculturists the bird is now being released again in its native state.

Truly, the Bahaman Amazon must be allowed to get into the aviaries of dedicated aviculturists who will do a reliable job in reproducing the bird to a point where it, too, will be with us forever. The human population is affecting the rare birds so much that something must be done in addition to

Mealy Amazon, *Amazona farinosa farinosa.* All mealy Amazons have yellow on the front and forecrown.

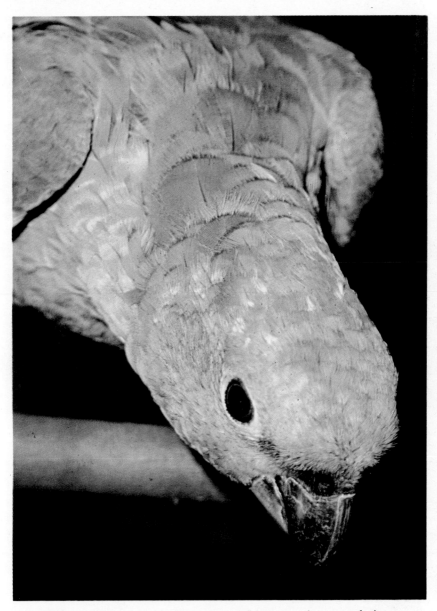

Close-up of the head of a blue-crowned Amazon, *Amazona farinosa guatemalae.*

opening up national wildlife refuges.

On my trip to the Bahamas I visited Great Inagua Island, where one could see flocks of a dozen Bahaman Amazons flying overhead to search for food. It is hoped that a sight such as this occurs for a long time. Perhaps with the new laws involving their protection they will fly longer. On the island of Abaco (which I did not visit), there seems to be a desire on the part of the populace to protect the Bahaman Amazon.

To the best of my knowledge, there are no Bahaman Amazons in the United States.

GRAND CAYMAN AMAZON
Amazona leucocephala caymanensis

This subspecies is extensively heard and found on Grand Cayman Island. They are more yellowish green in color, with less black scalloping on each feather. In addition, the white on the forehead and crown is similar to that on the Santo Domingo or present to a lesser extent than in the Cuban. The beautiful rose color extends down the throat to the upper breast, as in the Cuban. There is a small eye ring about the eye, with white feathers as well as some rose-colored feathers. A rich maroon or wine color is seen in the lower abdomen, again as in the Cuban.

A.l. caymanensis is the second largest subspecies of the group involving the Cuban, Grand Cayman, Brac Cayman, Bahaman and Isle of Pines Amazons. I have observed that the Grand Cayman Amazon is somewhat sexually dimorphic by symmetrical lines; that is, the female's head is somewhat more rounded than the male's. This is not so in the Cuban Amazon.

A.l. caymanensis is found on the Grand Cayman Islands

in groups of six to forty. They are comparatively quiet, feeding mostly on flowers and fruits. There are a couple of good pet Grand Cayman Amazons in Connecticut and at least one breeder in Florida with success but there are very few Grand Cayman Amazons in the United States.

CAYMAN BRAC AMAZON
Amazona leucocephala hesterna

This subspecies is dwindling extremely fast. Friends on Cayman Brac have indicated that there are no more than fifty of these birds left. There appears to be none on Little Cayman Island.

This subspecies is smaller than the Cuban Amazon; it is indeed the smallest of the *Amazona leucocephala* subspecies. The color of this bird is close to that of the Cuban, with the exception of the rose coloring. The rose is confined to the cheek area in the Cayman Brac; in some individuals it goes to the throat area, but even so it is much less defined than in the Cuban. The lower abdomen is invariably more orchid or purplish than the usual maroon seen in the Cuban or Grand Cayman.

The Cayman Brac Amazon has an unusually large eye ring in comparison to the Grand Cayman and the Cuban. Almost always one sees distinct white feathers around this eye ring, whereas in the Grand Cayman and Cuban some rose feathers are seen on the much smaller eye ring.

As far as this writer knows, only one breeder of the Cayman Brac exists in the United States. Laurels should go to the few breeders in the world who have been successful in reproducing this rare Amazon. Perhaps only those birds bred in captivity will be evident in future years, because the wild population is in great danger. Unlike the Bahaman

A pair of plain-colored Amazons, *Amazona farinosa inornata.* These are large Amazons with no yellow on or about their heads. Many people feel that this Amazon's common name is a misnomer; it is plain in color but nonetheless exquisite.

Right: festive Amazon, *Amazona festiva festiva.* Below: plain-colored Amazon, *A. farinosa inornata.*

169

Amazon, which is now protected, the Cayman Brac Amazon is looked upon as a nuisance. This puts it in greater jeopardy.

CUBAN AMAZON
Amazona leucocephala leucocephala

While studying parrots at the Mayaguez, Puerto Rico Zoological Gardens, I was amazed at the truly beautiful colors of the Cuban Amazon parrot. This zoo has a tremendous collection of parrots, including one breeding pair of Cubans. All parrots at this zoo had sufficient flight space and the necessary hollow logs or similar nest sites. A most suitable nest was available to the pair of unbelievable Cubans.

The Cuban Amazon is extremely rare in the United States, although this writer knows of at least two breeders housing one or more pairs. Although the pair at Mayaguez had not produced young, they provided a good subject for study.

The Cuban is larger than the Santo Domingo Amazon, but not so much larger that there is a major difference in size; the Cuban is only slightly larger.

The main characteristic of the Cuban Amazon involves the striking rose color of the throat, neck and upper abdomen. Only seeing is believing, as this color is fascinating. The lower abdomen contains green feathers intermingled with rose feathers, gradually becoming maroon in color and giving a hue of very low maroon character. As in the Santo Domingo, the green feathers are edged in black. Ear coverts are black; the forehead and crown, however, are a distinct white. In comparison, the crown of the Cuban is more starkly white than that of the Santo Domingo. The primary

Cuban Amazon.

Diademed Amazon, *Amazona autumnalis diadema.*

Wood's lilac-crowned Amazon, *Amazona finschi woodi.*

and secondary feathers are a dull blue color although edged in green. Tail feathers are green with yellow, red and blue. Tail coverts are yellowish green.

The first Amazon to be seen in Europe was the beautiful Cuban. Early explorers brought this Amazon back with them for presentation to royalty. Many of these fabulous Amazons became excellent talkers and of utmost importance to royalty as high-class items.

Little is known about the status of the Cuban Amazon today in its homeland, since few persons interested in birds have visited Cuba in recent years.

ISLE OF PINES AMAZON
Amazona leucocephala palmarum

From the Isle of Pines just south of Cuba comes a rare Amazon, *Amazona leucocephala palmarum*. This subspecies is darker green in color than the Cuban; the rose is a darker rose-red. The maroon of the lower abdomen is almost purple in color. We are told that this color is sometimes not as distinct as some writers may indicate. The Isle of Pines Amazon is exceedingly rare in the United States but has been bred by one or more individuals with success.

Cal Sharp of Iowa had a mated pair of Isle of Pines Amazons that he kept for thirty-two years. Cal is now in his seventies and loves to talk about this pair, the favorite parrots of his career in aviculture. These birds were taken by Cal on the Isle of Pines when he lived in Cuba years ago. He hand-raised the babies to tame adults. They talked continuously, displaying the antics typical of a comical parrot. They teased the household cat by biting her tail. They rode on the back of the family Chihuahua; they ate breakfast with Cal and his wife and loved to perch on Cal's shoulder, both at the same time. Most interesting is that they were male and female from different nests, and they raised no fewer than four clutches of babies in the years Cal kept those two fine birds. It was a very sad day after thirty-two years for Cal to lose the female one day and the male exactly six months later. To this day Cal feels badly that he did not retain some of the young birds. He has not been able to secure an Isle of Pines Amazon since the loss of his two.

GRAY-NAPED AMAZON
Amazona mercenaria canipalliata

Nothing is known about the avicultural aspects of the gray-naped Amazon, although it is evidently fairly plentiful in the western mountains of Bolivia. This Amazon apparently loves higher elevations.

Like the scaly-naped Amazon, this bird is most shy and difficult for the natives to collect. Accordingly, the few collections made have been for skins for various museums. Collections for live specimens have been very few indeed.

All Amazons nest in hollow trees of one type or another. They use old woodpecker holes by excavating them more. They utilize all types of trees, from the acacia to the cabbage palm. Amazon parrot eggs are always solid white, half the size of bantam chicken eggs. They generally hatch in 26 to 28 days. Amazons lay from two to four eggs generally, but more often it is two. On rare occasions, natives of certain islands have indicated that they have seen a nest of five or six eggs. This would be unusual. I did see one nest in the mountains of Hispaniola containing six baby Santo Domingo Amazons. I was shocked into almost disbelief. To this day I feel that there was some human manipulation involved. The gray-naped Amazon is the most elusive of all

Wood's lilac-crowned Amazon is occasionally referred to as Wood's Amazon.

Opposite:
Escaped Amazons in a royal palm tree. The Amazon near the trunk is a Finsch's, while the other is a white-fronted.

Amazons; nothing is known of its nesting habits.

I have seen no records of importations of the gray-naped Amazon and I have seen but one gray-naped Amazon. This bird was in a collection in Mexico in the late 1960's. The owners did not know what they had except that it was an Amazon.

SCALY-NAPED AMAZON
Amazona mercenaria mercenaria

Rare in avicultural circles but plentiful in the wild, the scaly-naped Amazon is one of the forgotten Amazons. It is literally all green except for the wings and tail. For this reason, this Amazon is not as desirable as the others.

Of course, I think all Amazons are beautiful. In western Venezuela, where the scaly-naped Amazon is plentiful but comparatively quiet (at least in comparison to most other Amazons), local natives believe they are beautiful and elusive.

The crown and nape are green with black edging, which accounts for the scaly-naped name. Occasionally the bend of the wing is red and yellow, while the primaries and secondaries are green with blue-violet ends. The base of the outer three secondaries is bright red. The tail is colorful. The two outer tail feathers are purple. The base of the lateral feathers is green, with red centers and yellow-green ends. The central tail feathers are green, tipped in greenish yellow.

I have seen no records of importations into the United States. Likewise, I do not know of a zoo, aviculturist or pet owner who has a scaly-naped Amazon. The only three I have ever seen were from a group of five Amazons owned by a Javan family in Surinam. These Amazons were much more attractive than I had surmised. We were enjoying a luscious Javanese meal while watching the antics of the parrots. The other two were *Amazona ochrocephala ochrocephala*, the yellow-fronted Amazon.

Several bird skins taken on expeditions to Bolivia have been studied. All skins were surprisingly similar, with very few differentiations. Only Natterer's Amazon has shown such consistency between skins in my studies.

In its home area this bird has the reputation of being very timid and hard to collect.

YELLOW-NAPED AMAZON
Amazona ochrocephala auropalliata

One of the most symmetrical of all Amazons, of all parrots in fact, is the yellow-naped Amazon. I truly believe that this Amazon is the best choice for all people. They are better as talkers, their antics are clownish, their intelligence is superb and, as mentioned above, I've yet to see one that is not symmetrically outstanding. All are well shaped, and all yellow-napes can show off well. One effective characteristic involves the fanning of the tail. They show well when the tail is well fanned. Many Amazons will fan or spread their tails, but none performs better than the yellow-naped Amazon.

The forehead and crown of the yellow-nape is a distinct dark green. A yellow band which varies from bird to bird can be seen on the nape of the neck. Wings appear green at the bend; definitely no red or yellow appears at the bend of the wing. Primaries and secondaries are green at the base and blue at the ends. Secondaries have red at bases of each feather. Tail feathers are dark green at the base, extending to a light yellow green. Thighs are light green. The yellow

Cuban Amazon, *Amazona leucocephala leucocephala.*

Opposite:
Close-up of a Cuban
Amazon's head.

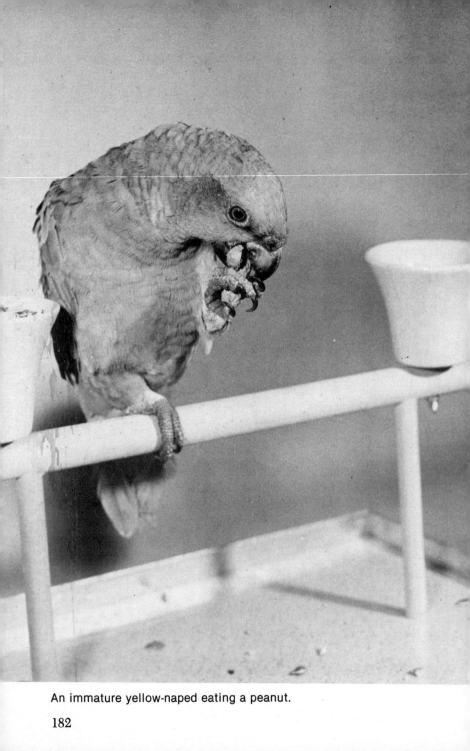

An immature yellow-naped eating a peanut.

182

nape and dark gray or black bill are the oustanding characteristics of this Amazon.

When I was living in Puerto Rico, a couple in their middle fifties brought in a large, personable, nice-looking yellow-naped Amazon for me to examine. As their story progressed, it was revealed that this particular bird was one hundred and three years of age. I had every reason to believe that this was correct. They had documentation of the bird's age that dated back to 1933. The bird had definite characteristics which depicted old age; one in particular was a benign tumor on the forehead, above the beak.

The current owner stated that when he was a young boy he well remembered this parrot going through antics at his aunt's home. It seems that his aunt lived in New York City. Some years previous to the birth of the current owner, this aunt had received this parrot as a gift from her boyfriend. The boyfriend had previously received the bird from his first lover, a burlesque queen. She, in turn, had received the yellow-naped Amazon from her long time boyfriend, a gallant bullfighter from Mexico. All of these personalities had long since passed to their hereafters, but the aunt willed the yellow-nape to this present owner. So here 50 years or so later was this 103-year-old bird—still going strong. He had a fabulous vocabulary, mostly Spanish.

My experiences with yellow-napes has been rewarding and interesting. One yellow-nape called Carmelita swore as if that was all she had ever heard or desired to pick up. It got so bad that we had to put her away or cover her cage whenever company would come. Fortunately, at the time, we had no children. Finally, a neighborhood farmer requested Carmelita so frequently that we relented and sold her to him. Little did we know that he was planning to open a bar room; she became a permanent fixture.

Yellow-napes will almost always do well in a bird show. They show well, they constantly talk, they fan their tails well and repeatedly fascinate the judge. One interesting

Charlie, a yellow-naped Amazon, displaying himself.

Opposite:
A close-up of the head of a
yellow-naped Amazon, *Amazona
ochrocephala auropalliata.*

yellow-naped Amazon decided she was going to lay two eggs in the bottom of her cage. She refused to let her owner remove these eggs for a long period. She incubated the eggs constantly with no success of course, since she was an only bird for a long period of time. Finally she relented; the owner removed the eggs. She graciously presented the man two eggs each year but never let them go for at least six weeks each time.

Another friend of ours had a beautiful, well balanced pair of yellow-naped Amazons. They had been in his possession for ten years at the time of our first discussion concerning their breeding background and problems. It seems that on four successive occasions the female had laid two eggs and properly incubated them with successful hatching only to kill the young when they were about four weeks of age. How distressing to the owner!

I questioned the owner about the diet of the birds during incubation and while the fledglings were developing. Bob had fed sunflower and safflower seeds, peanuts, apples, oranges, bananas and grapes. Undoubtedly the problem was lack of good meat protein. Little is known of the diet of Amazons in the wild, particularly when nesting. My Amazons and macaws love meat. Sure, a little at a time—but meat is a must.

Bob started giving canned dog food containing red meat to the pair. In due time the hen laid three eggs (which was a first). She incubated these eggs; two of them hatched. Bob increased the amount of meat protein fed; for the first time two babies had fledged. We cannot stress enough to each of you breeders: *feed meat protein to your breeders!*

I have said that the best-talking Amazon, in general, is the yellow-naped. A professor at a midwestern university who was also a good friend and fellow dog breeder had repeatedly stated his yellow-naped Amazon had a vocabulary of three hundred words, could sing *Yankee Doodle* and the *Star Spangled Banner* and loved to recite the

Yellow-naped Amazon, Amazona ochrocephala auropalliata.

187

This double yellow-head Amazon, *Amazona ochrocephala oratrix,* is obviously irritated.

Opposite:
Panama Amazon,
Amazona ochrocephala panamensis

189

alphabet in French. This was difficult to accept, but in due time it was proved to me. The professor had not only placed me in a precarious position for me to watch and hear, but he also taped an extensive conversation of a bird—a magnificent yellow-naped Amazon.

If I were approached by a stranger asking my opinion on the type of Amazon to purchase, I would probably suggest the yellow-naped. My suggestion would be candid, even though the plain-colored Amazon is closest to my heart.

BELIZE AMAZON
Amazona ochrocephala belizensis

Another of the yellow-headed Amazons that is rarely seen and, when seen, is often confused with *A.o. oratrix* is the Belize Amazon. As previously noted, this Amazon is found only in British Honduras, now called Belize. The front, crown, upper cheeks and ear coverts are yellow, with a few yellow feathers scattered on the nape and throat. Too often this Amazon is called the double yellow-head. It is a smaller bird than *A.o. oratrix* by two to three inches. With training and study, one can develop an expertise in differentiating the two subspecies.

Perhaps the best place to pick out a Belize is at a bird show where numerous "double yellow-heads" are exhibited. Fairly often one will note the appearance of at least one smaller bird with less yellow about the nape and throat. At one eastern show at which I was judging, there was a tremendous class of double yellow-heads, perhaps a dozen. This was a good class of Amazons, well represented by generally good, large, colorful birds. There was one, however, that was less colorful and smaller, which I would classify as a Belize. Normally most judges will put a smaller, less colorful bird down to a more colorful, larger Amazon if all other conditions such as feather quality and steadiness are equal.

It is difficult to state that the Belize should be classified in a different section from *A.o. oratrix* or Tres Marias, since the normal classifier cannot differentiate the three. It becomes a matter of fate that they are placed in competition together; nine times out of ten a Tres Marias has it over an *A.o. oratrix* while an *A.o. oratrix* has it over a Belize. Then, of course, occasionally an *A.o. magna* is involved. This bird is a duplicate of *A.o. oratrix*, but two to three inches larger. I strongly believe that with study and much patience one can differentiate between each of these so-called double yellow-heads. (Keep in mind that *A.o. oratrix* is the true double yellow-head Amazon.)

LARGE OR MAGNA DOUBLE YELLOW-HEAD AMAZON
Amazona ochrocephala magna

An exceptionally large double yellow-head Amazon, two to three inches larger than *Amazona ochrocephala oratrix*, this bird from southern Mexico rivals the Tres Marias Amazon in size and beauty. If anything, the magna lacks some of the yellow color that the Tres Marias exhibits and seems to be a darker green in general body color. Not all ornithologists consider this bird sufficiently different from *A.o. oratrix* to be classed as a separate subspecies, but I think it should be and will treat it as such.

Besides being large, *A.o. magna* is also colorful, as colorful as *A.o. oratrix*. When exhibited, this Amazon's size and beauty are difficult to beat if all other conditions are equal. At the 1977 New Hampshire Cagebird show, with over one

Janet Lilienthal and Billy, her protector, a double yellow-head Amazon.

Opposite:
Top: close-up of a double yellow-headed Amazon, *Amazona ochrocephala oratrix. Below:* One can easily distinguish the red-lored from the double yellow-head.

193

hundred parrots exhibited in many classes, I selected Best Double Yellow-Head from a group of seven entered. The winner was a faultless *A.o. magna*. This bird was elevated to Best Amazon over several other top Amazons, including a superb Rothschild's and a strong·class of orange-wings. By the time the magna was chosen as Best South American Parrot, most observers in the gallery had selected it as their favorite. In due time it defeated an outstanding cockatiel, an Indian ringneck and a rare mutation parrot for Best Parrot in the show, finally going all the way to Best Bird in the show. This bird is truly a magnificent and large double yellow-headed Amazon; unfortunately, most readers will never be fortunate enough to see a magna, much less own one. Remember, however, that the true double yellow-head is *Amazona ochrocephala oratrix*.

NATTERER'S AMAZON
Amazona ochrocephala natterer

This Amazon has confused many persons, even top taxonomists. In previous decades, many writers, both laymen and ornithologists, have classified Natterer's Amazon as a blue-fronted Amazon, *Amazona aestiva aestiva*, while others believed it to be *Amazona ochrocephala ochrocephala*, the yellow-front Amazon.

We believe that today's classification is correct, since the conformation and symmetrical balance of Natterer's Amazon make it more closely resemble other members of the species *Amazona ochrocephala*.

The color differences are most interesting; this is the only *Amazona ochrocephala* subspecies exhibiting a bluish color about the head. It differs from *Amazona ochrocephala ochrocephala* by having a frontal band which is extremely broad and is green with strong bluish suffusion. The cheeks, ear coverts and throat also appear to have this bluish green color. It is a type of suffusion. There is definitely no yellow on the sides of the head. This subspecies is much larger than the yellow-front Amazon, *Amazona ochrocephala ochrocephala.*

My study of bird skins at the Los Angeles County Museum of Natural History proved interesting. Several specimens were examined. All, were very much alike in conformation and color. I have not examined any other group of major Amazon skins that were so well matched to each other, even though the skins came from several different areas.

Very few Natterer's Amazons are seen in trade channels of importers and dealers. Evidently, not too many are imported. Occasionally, they are sold as large blue-front Amazons.

I have seen a large, beautiful specimen exhibited at Busch Gardens in Los Angeles. This bird is most attractive and is very tame. When studying the characteristics of Natterer's Amazon, one can hardly help but wish to own a specimen, yet I only know of one pair of Natterer's Amazons in captivity within an aviculturist's breeding realm. Our female aviculturist friend owned this pair for sixteen years. Year after year she attempted to breed them, using proper nesting procedures, adequate feeding and top care. She was certain by their actions that they were male and female. Upon the entrance into an era of surgical sexing, our friend decided to check out her theory and have the pair of Natterer's categorized. The outcome was astounding; she had two females! Regardless of how sure you may be as to the sex of your Amazons, regardless of how affectionate a "pair" of Amazons seem, regardless of whether they regurgitate to feed each other, they still may be the same sex.

Fanciers who have only a single Amazon may be lucky. They have no need to breed their birds since they want them only as pets. However, time after time, I have known

A double yellow-head taking a bath.

Opposite:
A double yellow-head
displaying excellent color.

owners of one bird who, to their amazement find an egg at the bottom of the cage. The one nice thing about that is that if it happens you can be *sure* you have a female.

YELLOW-FRONTED AMAZON
Amazona
ochrocephala ochrocephala

The frontal area of this Amazon is yellow, with an extremely narrow green band on the frontal edge of the forehead. Most yellow-fronts do not have a yellow crown. In very young birds, very little yellow is detected on the frontal area.

The crown, nape and back feathers are dark green; slightly tipped edges of black occur. Upper tail coverts and feathers of the lower breast and abdomen are yellowish green. There is some red at the bend of the wing and red at the base of the tail. The wing speculum is red.

While visiting in Surinam I was able to view many young-caught specimens being prepared for export to Holland. Most of these Amazons had either a small amount of yellow on the front or no yellow at all. On an expedition to the interior of Surinam, I noted the birds' selection of wooded areas in higher elevations. Huge flocks of these Amazons appeared to feed in the manicole palms.

Our guide looked for termite nests in which he located yellow-front Amazon nests. These nests almost always contained either two babies or two eggs.

It bothered me to see the collectors of young birds cut down trees just to remove the young Amazons. I wondered whether the parent birds would be fortunate enough to locate another nesting hole on another occasion of breeding or be able to use the termite nesting areas. Our hosts indicated that hundreds of nesting areas still occurred in the jungles of Surinam and other related countries.

In the midst of the jungles of Surinam was a large quarantine station with hundreds of young yellow-front Amazons. These birds were destined to be shipped from Paramaribo to Holland.

I fully expected to see more parrots flying along the jungle road during the 30-mile trek to the airport from the capital city, but none were seen. At the airport, however, were two families, each having a pair of yellow-fronted Amazons destined for some long journey.

Hundreds of yellow-fronted Amazons have been imported into the United States in the past five years, yet where they have gone is a mystery to me. They are neither as beautiful as the double yellow-head nor as symmetrical as the yellow-naped nor as talkative as the yellow-crowned. I know of a few so-called singletons in private homes, but not a single pair of these Amazons is set up for breeding in the many aviaries I have visited. Surely there must be several. This species has been successfully bred in both England and the United States.

An associate in New York City, John Caroni, owns a yellow-fronted Amazon parrot as well as a turtle. While released (and this is most of the time), the bird spends a large portion of its time perching on the shell of the turtle. Whether the turtles realizes it has a companion is not known. The turtle will go about its business, even to the point of eating vegetation with no apparent hesitation or attentiveness to the presence of noisy Pedro. Pedro has developed an excellent vocabulary. His favorite expression is "Whoa" or "Get Up," followed by a sharp whistle. His antics are amplified by nipping at the ears of the family toy poodle. The poodle, however, seems to enjoy the little pest, particularly since Pedro likes to spend most of his time on the turtle.

It is noted that more yellow-front Amazons were im-

Left: this is an
unusual mutation of
A. o. panamensis.

The subspecies of *Amazona ochrocephala* fall into three main groups: yellow covering the entire head, yellow on the nape, and yellow only on the front of the head. Of the third group, those with yellow fronts, the most common subspecies are *A. o. ochrocephala* and *A. o. panamensis*. Very often the characters exhibited by a single individual will be contradictory: some associate the bird with *ochrocephala,* while others point to *panamensis.* I have found that these two subspecies can best be distinguished by the amount of yellow between the front and the crown; in short, yellow extending onto the top of the head indicates the subspecies *panamensis.* Thus the photograph above does not allow subspecific identification, while the amazon on the facing page (below) belongs to the subspecies *panamensis.*

ported into the country in 1977 than any other type of parrot with the exception of the nanday conure. In the Los Angeles area alone there were 15,000 or more imported.

DOUBLE YELLOW-HEAD AMAZON
Amazona ochrocephala oratrix

The double yellow-head Amazon is perhaps the best known of the Amazons and perhaps also one of the best talkers among them. It is probably the most beautiful of all Amazons as well, particularly when in full adult color. This would most definitely be at about twenty-five years of age.

This subspecies' color is exemplified by a lustrous yellow at the front, crown and nape of the neck throughout to the throat area. This yellow is carried through to the foreneck on many subspecies. The back is a dark green; the breast and vent area is a lighter green. The bend of the wing is orange-red, fading to a distinct yellow. Primary and secondary feathers are basically green, fading to bluish black tips. Some red is visible in the secondary wing feathers. The tail feathers are tipped with green. The under tail is heavily marked with red and some blue. Legs and beak are generally gray, but some are yellowish.

Amazona ochrocephala oratrix is restricted in range to Mexico; in fact Mexico is identified with the bird to the extent that it is often called the Mexican double yellow-head instead of just plain double yellow-head. The range of many other Amazon subspecies crosses national boundaries, but *A.o. oratrix* stays within one country.

Very few parrots are better talkers than the double yellow-head. We know of one that was purchased by a friend in Ohio as a youngster—within just a few weeks it could repeat its name fluently, saying "Tito, Tito," and its vocabulary is growing.

Another friend owns two double yellow-heads. One is twenty-eight years of age; the other is about seven. The first one has spoken with great clarity over 120 words. She cries like a baby, barks like a dog, laughs, whistles and sings. The younger bird is already mimicking "Petsy" with a vocabulary almost as spectacular.

My own "Pedro" was a card! He loved to dance about his open perch whistling as though he were the only one in the world who could emit the wolf whistle. He loved to say "I'm a parrot, I'm a parrot." He also picked up another word, unfortunately unprintable. We honestly wonder how he could have picked it up, since we never utter it. We had purchased him for fifty dollars in the late 1950's. He was very young, having yellow only about the crown and front of the head. When we went overseas in 1970 we had to give him up. It was most difficult. Before we parted with Pedro we purchased a mate for him. We were informed that "Maria" was a Tres Marias Amazon (which will be later discussed) and that she was a seasoned breeder.

We placed Pedro and Maria in a large flight about six feet high, six feet long and six feet wide. In it we placed a beautiful (to a bird breeder) hollow apple tree log. This was to no avail, for in two straight years they never once approached the log. Maria was found dead one morning in the corner of the flight cage. On post-mortem it was noted that her liver was greatly enlarged and loaded with abscesses. Testicles were also found; Maria was a male.

We tried again with the purchase of another female. This one was owned by an elderly lady; she had had the double yellow-head for ten years. She indicated that "Posey" had laid one egg on the cage floor two years previously. Sure enough, within three weeks after Pedro and Posey were finally placed together, Posey was showing interest in the

Feral Amazon in the vicinity of Miami, Florida. Field observers census this species, *Amazona ochrocephala,* as the "Yellow-headed Amazon."

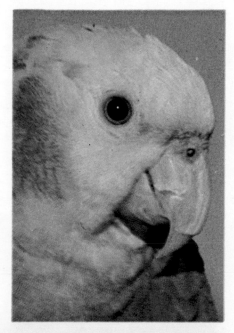

Right: Close-up of a young Tres Marias Amazon, *Amazona ochrocephala tresmariae.* *Below:* A double yellow-head and a blue-fronted.

205

log. (Prior to Posey's release into the pen, it was extremely important to place her in direct sight of Pedro so they could become friendly through caging. This prevents unnecessary fighting and killing.) Posey's interest in the log continued for well over a year. Pedro gained interest only gradually during this long time. Posey would enter the nest hole and remain for long periods of time.

We dare not peek too frequently into nesting areas, but we did in this case. One day in July we peeked with excitement and enthusiasm to see four eggs in the nesting hole. This was truly a delight; it was an occurrence that seems to happen only once in a lifetime (at least at the time of the occurrence). We dared not peek again into the nest.

We decided to increase the variety of foods offered during the nesting season. In addition to sunflower seeds we increased the amount of fruit by placing diced apples, diced bananas and grapes into the feed hopper. White pound cake was especially made for this pair. We also fed many portions of endive and dandelion greens. We were determined that we would overcome the problem encountered by other breeders of Amazons; that is, if we were fortunate enough to secure a hatch—even one chick would electrify us, and we would save it.

Through the extremely long three or four weeks of incubation, the male never entered the nest hole. He would regurgitate to the female on her appearance at the nest hole edge. She would also emerge to take food periodically.

After what seemed to be an endless wait, we were sure we could hear noises within the nest that sounded as if babies were present. The parents became so mean and protective that we could no longer enter the flight cage. So there we were, sure that we had some baby parrots but unable to see how many. We continued feeding a great variety of food, keeping in mind that many friends over the years had been successful in breeding the double yellow-head, hatching the chicks and watching them thrive—only to see the parents literally butcher them when they are 3 to 4 weeks of age.

My theory is that because of a metabolism rate that changes considerably in adult parrots while they are feeding their babies, the parents lack in protein, so they actually destroy their chicks. In order to prevent this occurrence, we started feeding canned dog food to the adults. Surprisingly, they loved it. After a three-week wait we were able to peek quickly into the nest. There we saw a beautiful sight—four ugly baby parrots.

Almost sixty days later the baby Amazons started to emerge from the nest hole. We were greatly surprised to see very little yellow about their heads. At this time we removed them from the parents to insure that we would tame them as excellent pets. We were successful. All four became excellent hand-tamed double yellow-head parrots. To this day they are still alive in homes filled with love and a fine parrot environment.

Indeed, the double yellow-head is a real talker. At times it is amazing to listen to their mimicry. It seems that they not only learn how to mimic but also sometimes use logic. Pedro had the ability to detect conditions and utter statements that were awesome. For example, one wintry day we had a heavy snowstorm. Pedro repeatedly stated, "It's snowing. It's snowing," yet he never uttered these words in the spring, summer or fall.

Posey loved to take baths. She would bathe in an inch of water as well as a foot of water. She would throw the water around with her beak and spray further using her wings. She seemed to enjoy giving nearby people a bath.

At the bird shows, you will see more double yellow-head Amazons than any other Amazon. They always exhibit themselves in top fashion, talking away in either their language or ours.

Beauty is in color and is beheld by all. Those greens, yellows and reds make this subspecies truly exquisite.

The comparative sizes of different parrots. (Scale ¼ actual size) 1. greater sulphur-crested cockatoo; 2. African gray parrot; 3. Finsch's Amazon; 4. yellow-naped Amazon; 5. blue and yellow macaw; 6. blue-headed parrot; 7. blue-fronted Amazon; 8. roseate or rose-breasted cockatoo;

9. blue wing parrotlet; 10. lineolated parakeet; 11. Tovi parakeet; 12. Petz' conure; 13. yellow-fronted Amazon; 14. green-cheeked Amazon; 15. spectacled Amazon; 16. golden-crowned conure. (Drawing by R. A. Vowles)

PANAMA OR
YELLOW-CROWNED AMAZON
Amazona ochrocephala panamensis

The Panama Amazon is one of the most spectacular of the Amazons. They are louder and extremely intelligent. They are also more confused in people's minds than any other Amazon I have seen. Too many of them are confused with yellow-napes; others are confused with yellow-fronts. They can be differentiated from *Amazona o. ochrocephala* by their having bright yellow on the frontal area, crown and lores. Small brownish hairy feathers about the nostrils are also evident. There is some red at the bend of the wing, but not as much as is seen on the bend of the wing of *Amazona ochrocephala oratrix*. Many persons strongly believe that the Panama Amazon is the best talker of all Amazons and, indeed, all parrots. Certainly one that this writer owns has a steady but sometimes rapidly enunciated vocabulary. Oscar, as he is called, is the most lovable parrot in the eyes of our many guests and aviculturists. He steals the show by constantly jabbering in both English and Spanish. He loves to strut along his perch cackling like a hen that has just laid an egg. Immediately after, he utters the most fascinating "cock-a-doodle doo." He perfectly mimics a tiny bantam rooster.

Oscar loves to loudly cry "Arriba, Arriba!!" Somewhere along the way, this Panama Amazon learned to mimic Lolita, the popular yellow-naped Amazon that actively participates in the bird show at the San Diego Wild Animal Park. Our male repeats in extremely loud tones "Lolita, Lolita."

The female in the same aviary as Oscar is almost as complete in vocabulary. She also cackles like a hen, although she does not crow like a rooster. Apparently she leaves the

Amazona ochrocephala: the yellow extending from the cere onto the crown indicates the subspecies *panamensis.*

Santo Domingo Amazon, *Amazona ventralis.*

The Santo Domingo Amazon is also known as the Hispaniolan Amazon.

crowing to the male. We call her Sanchita. She repeats her name continually while fanning her tail and raising her hackles or nape feathers.

This pair was moved two hundred miles in a station wagon during a hot day in June. Only two days later, the female laid one egg in a *cockatiel type nest box* (only smaller). Both Panamas were housed in an aviary 6 feet x 4 feet x 4 feet. Within a few days we peeked to see just how many eggs this Panama did lay; there were three.

In twenty-seven days my son checked the nest box and in disbelief he noted that one baby Amazon had hatched. I had to look myself to believe it, since I was sure the long trip just prior to her laying was most certainly a stress on her. Sure enough, we had a baby Panama. The other two eggs did not hatch.

We immediately initiated a feeding program to induce the parents to feed the baby well. We had decided that the baby would remain with the parents if at all possible. Each day we offered corn on the cob, bread (whole wheat) and milk, cheese, monkey chow, sunflower and millet seeds, bananas, apples, apple sauce, black bread and dog food in two different forms. The first thing devoured each time was the cheese, then the bread and milk. With a flashlight we could occasionally look into the nest box to see the progress of the baby. Pinfeathers did not appear until the twentieth day. We thought this was unusually slow. The young Panama opened its eyes on the thirteenth day, however. The remaining feathers came in rapidly, with back feathers coming in the last and the slowest. However, we were suspicious that the mother was pulling out some of the back feathers.

The parents were excellent feeders; the female remained in the nest box almost constantly. We were pleased to see complete fledging of the youngster on the forty-fifth day. He came out of the nest frequently and perched beside his parents. We named the curious little fellow "Ichabod."

It is noteworthy to mention that meat was consumed in much greater amounts as the baby became three and four weeks of age. We believe the success in raising this baby Amazon was directly related to the amount of meat consumed by the parents. They must have high protein to raise young. "Ichabod" developed into a beautiful large Panama Amazon; he has become extremely tame and gentle and already has an extensive vocabulary.

SMALL YELLOW-NAPED AMAZON
Amazona ochrocephala parvipes

Most of the yellow-naped Amazons imported into the United States during the late 1970's are of the subspecies *Amazona ochrocephala auropalliata*; *A.o. parvipes* is noticeably smaller. Red at the bend of the wing is the other chief difference in appearance. Extremely young birds of both *A.o. parvipes* and *A.o. auropalliata* do not have any red at the bend of the wing; *A.o. parvipes*, the small yellow-naped, does have the red bend of the wing in adults. Young of both *A.o. parvipes* and *A.o. auropalliata* have no yellow on the nape until some age is seen. Often they are only distinguished as green Amazons with gray horny bills. *A.o. parvipes* has a much paler bill.

I have seen only one pair of *Amazona ochrocephala parvipes* in captivity in an aviary. I have seen an occasional individual in a pet shop, but the owners did not realize what they had. An avid aviculturist in Connecticut owns the pair of *A.o. parvipes*. They are small and as exquisite as yellow-naped Amazons. He has indicated that this pair has been owned by him since 1968, at which time he purchased them at a ridiculously low price in Nicaragua. Mating is

Escaped Amazons in flight. The mixed flock includes *viridigenalis,* *albifrons,* and *ochrocephala* individuals.

Opposite:
Vinaceous Amazon,
Amazona vinacea.

quite frequent between these two birds; he claims that he has seen them mating in November by moonlight. He maintains these birds all year round in an outdoor aviary in Connecticut. They do have a shelter into which to retreat. He maintains them in a flight aviary with dimensions of 4 ft. x 15 ft. x 6 ft.

The female has successfully laid and hatched two eggs for three consecutive years, each time in July. This gentleman feeds the normal sunflower seeds, bread and milk sweetened with Karo syrup, pound cake and fried chicken. The breeding birds devour chicken almost in a cannibalistic manner.

His nestbox was a grandfather clock type with black soil on the bottom. The belief at this aviary is that the parents do the best job feeding the young. Many will debate this, and I have seen success both ways, but if one has the time there is much benefit derived from hand-feeding young parrots.

TRES MARIAS AMAZON
Amazona ochrocephala tresmariae

Perhaps one of the most beautiful of the subspecies in the double yellow-head group is the Tres Marias Amazon. There is definitely more yellow on the entire head and throat, extending down onto the neck and breast. The back and wings are lighter green than those of *Amazona ochrocephala oratrix*. The bend of the wing has much red mixed with yellow; the thighs are a rich golden yellow. This is a larger bird with a longer tail than that of *A.o. oratrix*.

Very few people realize what they have when they indeed do have a Tres Marias. Of all the Amazons, the subspecies of *Amazona ochrocephala* can be the most confusing. Some of its members are extremely rare and beautiful, yet to the novice they are puzzling to differentiate.

The Tres Marias are a group of four islands off the coast of western Mexico. We understand that many Tres Marias Amazons can still be found on these islands.

We have one Tres Marias Amazon. One can compare this subspecies to a queen bee in a colony of honeybees. If you place a Tres Marias next to an *A.o. oratrix* there really is no contest. Our "Tressie" becomes more beautiful each succeeding year. She loves to talk and chuckle. She may literally talk to herself in low, chuckled tones for hours. For a bird to constantly entertain itself so well is a total delight. One problem exists, however: this Tres Marias does not like men. She (or maybe he—we can't be 100% certain) loves women, but she actively dislikes men.

This subspecies in particular is often thought to be and is sold under the name of double yellow-head Amazon. It is indeed a double yellow-head Amazon—but what a double yellow-head!!!

A certain pet shop in the middle west had a specialty of parrots and always kept several on hand. One particularly large and beautiful Amazon was advertised as a double yellow-head. A friend indicated to me that the bird in question was perhaps the most beautiful double yellow he had ever seen. I decided to accompany my friend to the pet shop with much eagerness. My suspicions were rewarded; this was a Tres Marias double yellow-head. The price was fabulous—extremely reasonable. My friend bought the bird on my advice.

When judging double yellow-head Amazons at various shows, I have occasionally noted a Tres Marias Amazon among the other less glamorous double yellow-heads. Inevitably they show better, look better and are classier. It takes an extremely outstanding normal double yellow-head to defeat the classy Tres Marias.

In 1972 I had made arrangements to purchase a Tres

A green-cheeked displaying his wings.

Opposite:
Free-flying green-cheeked
Amazons, *Amazona viridigenalis,*
in Florida.

Marias Amazon from a California aviculturist. This bird was to be accompanied by a chattering lory. I could hardly wait to receive those birds. One week before the shipping date, I was informed that California had blocked all shipments out of California. An outbreak of Newcastle disease had prevented all shipments out of California for a long time. Needless to say, I never did receive that Tres Marias Amazon.

In studying skins of Amazons at Peabody Museum at Yale University and also at the Los Angeles County Museum I was able to detect only one Tres Marias out of about forty *Amazona ochrocephala*. This bird was most colorful with yellow clear to the abdomen and down the nape of the neck to the middle of the back. The bend of the wings were deep red and yellow.

MARAJO YELLOW-HEADED AMAZON
Amazona ochrocephala xantholaema

On the island of Marajo at the mouth of the Amazon river is a yellow-headed Amazon, *Amazona ochrocephala xantholaema,* which differs little from the yellow-front Amazon, *Amazona ochrocephala ochrocephala*. In addition to having a narrow green frontal band and a yellow front, this Amazon parrot has an extensive amount of yellow on the sides of the head. The neck and upper back are green, with a black edging on each feather. The lower breast and abdomen are yellowish green. Tail coverts are yellow green, while the tail feathers end with a yellow-green band about 40% to the base of the feathers. The beak is dark gray, as are the legs.

Very few Marajo Amazons have been imported into the United States; I feel that since this subspecies ranges over a very small area, there will normally be only few importations.

Occasionally one sees a Marajo in a pet shop for sale as a double yellow-head Amazon. We do not ridicule this, since classifying the subspecies of *Amazona* species is often most difficult.

RED-SPECTACLED AMAZON
Amazona pretrei

Also called Pretre's Amazon, this true spectacled Amazon is very rare in the United States and, in fact, in aviculturists' collections throughout the world. In reviewing several collections of birdskins, I do not recall a single red-spectacled Amazon in any collection. Likewise, I know of no red-spectacled Amazons in private collections— although this certainly does not mean that none exist in avicultural or pet collections. (I was most surprised, for example, to find out that within ten miles of my aviary existed a large black palm cockatoo. It had been in residence for four years before we found out about it. The owners had joined a local bird club; through this club we learned of their fine collection. Another of their collection involved a fine looking red-tailed Amazon, even more rare in avicultural circles. So it is possible that someone, somewhere may possess a red-spectacled Amazon.)

I have only seen two living red-spectacled Amazons; they were well exhibited at the Mayaguez, Puerto Rico zoo a few years ago. They were most attractive birds. Their front was bright red extending through the crown and completely encircling the eye. Both birds had a few scattered red feathers

Hawkheaded Parrot.

throughout the green of the sides of the neck. Much red was evident at the bends of the wings, extending around to the primary coverts and primary feathers of the wing. Tails were green with yellow tips. Secondary feathers were blue and black. The hocks were rich in red and yellow. The general body color was green with black edging. Each of these Mayaguez birds that I describe had very yellow bills.

These two birds that were exhibited at the Mayaguez Zoo appeared very docile and very friendly. They clamored at the zoo fencing for full attention. I decided then to own a pair someday. Unfortunately, to date the opportunity has evaded me.

In reviewing several listings of imports as well as various brokers' price listings, I have never seen the red-spectacled Amazon listed. It is hoped that some individuals of the species will be made available for aviculturists to readily breed and reproduce so that this rare Amazon can be maintained.

TUCUMAN AMAZON
Amazona tucumana

Named after the province called Tucuman in Argentina, the Tucuman is an appealing Amazon. Seldom seen in the United States, this bird is very rarely imported. To the best of my knowledge, I know of no zoos now that house the Tucuman Amazon in the United States or its territories. Perhaps there are aviculturists or pet owners with an occasional Tucuman, but I have seen only one pair in captivity. That was some years ago at the Santo Domingo Zoo in the Dominican Republic.

It is evident that by studying birdskins one can appreciate the distinctive characteristics of particular species. So in

Vinaceous Amazon, *Amazona vinacea*. Photo by Harry V. Lacey.

the Tucuman I certainly appreciated the marked contrast in color of the hocks as compared to the hocks of most other Amazons. The hocks are a deep yellow, which is an appealing characteristic.

General body color is green; each feather is edged in black. The front is red; the crown and nape are green with black edgings on the feathers. On the wings the primaries are green, ending in blue at the tips. Primary coverts are red. Secondaries show blue with green. The tail is typical of most Amazons, being green with the tips a yellowish green.

This Amazon seems to be quite common in certain parts of Argentina and Bolivia, yet it is seldom exported. Of all the Amazons, this is the one that I have the least experience with, my only acquaintance coming from the few birdskins that I have studied.

SANTO DOMINGO AMAZON
Amazona ventralis

While on a visit to the Dominican Republic, my wife and I were allowed to travel to the mountains where many Santo Domingo Amazons are found flying freely about the upper elevations of the island Hispaniola, which holds both the Dominican Republic and the Republic of Haiti. The Haitians evidently dislike parrots as much as the Dominicans love them. One never sees a parrot in the homes or markets of Haiti, although many Santo Domingo Amazons are seen in homes and markets in the Dominican Republic.

On the trip to the mountains we were fortunate enough to see large flocks of the beautiful Santo Domingo Amazon. Our friend and guide found a nest with babies just recently fully feathered. There were six babies in a hollow acacia tree. (We later found out that human manipulators had moved a nest of three to this nest, which had originally held only three babies. Apparently the natives group babies in nests just before collecting them for sale at the markets.)

We watched these babies from a distance. I had not seen baby parrots in the wild being fed by parent birds. Soon one of the parents returned to the tree. We could hear the young make specific sounds similar to the *baa, baa* of a baby goat. It was so similar that one expected to see a goat or two in the area. The interesting aspect was how the parent fed the young chick by regurgitation. Our guide stated that there are generally two to four to a nest, but most generally there are three. The natives rob the nests of young when they are about five to seven weeks of age and feed them with a mixture of mashed banana and ground rice which has been pounded to a wet paste. At this age they are unable to eat hard seeds such as cracked corn. These young Amazons are delivered to the market in Santo Domingo, where they are placed in a large cage. They are then sold for the equivalent of ten American dollars each.

It is noted that many Puerto Ricans are bird lovers and travel to Santo Domingo frequently. Since it is illegal to bring birds back into Puerto Rico, ways have been developed to smuggle these Amazons into the commonwealth. One can purchase the parrot for ten dollars, a Dominican drum for two dollars and a tranquilizer for sixty cents. For another dollar, a young man will prepare the bird for you by administering the tranquilizer, taping the bird within the drum after making suitable airholes and then closing the drum. Needless to say we did not make a purchase. The market is a venture in itself. Besides numerous birds, all types of vegetables and foodstuffs are for sale in addition to objects of art, baskets and various herbs.

The Santo Domingo Amazon has a flashy horn-colored bill with a light cere. The front is generally white, but in some birds a few yellow feathers are detected at the base of the bill and just beneath the mandible of the chin. A few select birds have an occasional rose-colored feather or two in the area of the forehead and under the mandible. There is a distinct white eye ring encircling a black eye. Each ear covert has distinct black feathers that make up a circular appearance of black at each ear, just below the rear of each eye. The feathers of the crown, nape and back are a distinct bright green, each edged in black. This gives a scalloped appearance. Breast feathers are lighter green, becoming red, yellow and green towards the rear. Specifically, the lower abdomen is rich red maroon, a typical trait of the bird. Lower abdominal feathers have a yellowish green base halfway to the end. The other half is bright red with a green scalloped edge. This gives a beautiful mixture that varies in density from bird to bird. The same pattern is found on the feathers at hock level.

Wing primaries are dark blue on the fore side of each feather and black on the other side, giving a blue/black, blue/black effect. The last three primaries start showing green just before the blue. Secondaries are green on the front half and blue on the rear half, gradually turning more green as the secondary feathers become smaller. All wing coverts are green with black scalloped edges.

The tail is beautiful. Each tail feather is quartered in four colors: yellow, sky blue, red and light green. The vent area is bright yellowish green. This writer ponders over the variable amount of white in each bird. Some birds have a full inch of white on the forehead, while others have only a half or a quarter inch of white. Likewise we surmised that the yellow feathers of the front and chin were visible only on adults, but when we viewed some babies just fledged there were some yellow feathers.

As for the rose feathers, we strongly believe that they are the connecting link between the Santo Domingo Amazon and the beautiful Cuban Amazon. Indeed, they are close

Yellow-lored Amazon, *Amazona xantholora*. Photo courtesy Vogelpark Walsrode.

Amazona autumnalis diadema. Photo by Harry V. Lacey.

relatives. The entire chin, throat and upper breast of the Cuban are a beautiful rose color, and a pair of Cubans are a beautiful sight next to a pair of the lustrous Santo Domingo Amazons.

We have owned and bred Santo Domingo Amazons for many years, but our trip to the island of Hispaniola was indeed worthwhile to continue our learning process about Amazons.

The Santo Domingo is a small bird, only about two-thirds the size of a double yellow-head. We have some that talk quite well. One in particular has many antics typical of a clown. This particular bird speaks her Spanish name with enthusiasm. Since this bird was raised in a Spanish family, she was well versed in Spanish. "A como son las chinas? A como son las chinas?"—was one of her favorite sentences. Translated, this means "What is the price of oranges?" Cooka hated men, including me, but loved women and young boys. She loved to cling to Daren, my son. She would hang on to Daren's sweater and ride all over the yard with contentment. She loved to bark like a dog, ending with the usual "Cooka, Cooka." Evidently most Spanish-speaking people utilize the name Cooka as Americans use "Polly."

We have been successful in breeding the Santo Domingo Amazon (often also called the Hispaniolan Amazon). We have two true mated pairs; they each prefer a hollowed log for a nest in an enclosure about 4x4x4 feet. They do not appreciate company while courting, mating and nesting, so a canvas is used to "hide" them from any viewers.

Surprisingly, our Santo Domingo Amazons—so unlike wild birds of the species—have never produced over two eggs at any one time. The eggs hatch well, though.

Again, we believe the big clue in raising young parrots is the proper feeding of protein to the adults in the form of good meat. We feed it in the form of canned dog food; surprisingly, however, they do love to devour fried chicken.

The Santo Domingo parents have successfully reared three hatches with satisfaction and successful breeding. Invariably incubation lasted twenty-six days each time.

There aren't too many Santo Domingo Amazons in the United States. I know of four other breeders in Florida, Ohio, California and New York. Certainly there must be others, but they are very rare. Dr. William Wiseman, my good friend from Chillicothe, Ohio, is a well known breeder of the Santo Domingo. Dr. Wiseman has been known as a first-time breeder of several kinds of parrots, including the Guiana parrotlet. His studies of the Santo Domingo have been helpful to me.

ST. LUCIA AMAZON
Amazona versicolor

On a small island in the Lesser Antilles exists an endangered species of true parrot called the St. Lucia Amazon, named after its home island.

I was privileged to visit St. Lucia to study this splendid varicolored parrot. St. Lucia is 27 miles long and 14 miles wide, with some variations of width. It is about 110 miles northwest of Barbados and 20 miles south of Martinique.

We were guests of the various island authorities and stayed in the capital city of Castries, quite a quaint city. We couldn't wait to track through the rain forest and the jungles as far as the two lush, green-covered Pitons, two old volcanic mountains. We were awed by the vegetation of the jungle and the mountains. Banana plants were everywhere, giant taro leaves were always evident and, as in most Caribbean islands, the bougainvillea was magnificent.

Near the little village of Soufriere is a hotel called the Anse Chastenet Hotel which is surrounded by jungle and

Santo Domingo Amazon, also known as Hispaniolan Amazon, *Amazona ventralis*. Photo by Dr. Herbert R. Axelrod.

Yellow-naped Amazon, *Amazona ochrocephala auropalliata*. Photo by Dr. Herbert R. Axelrod.

perched on the side of a cliff. In this jungle I witnessed several St. Lucia Amazons feeding on various fruits. Surprisingly, they are not noisy when they feed. It was simply amazing that we could get so close to these beautiful birds. Eventually they did fly away, a group of about twenty, squawking away to the tops of the trees and headed toward the two Pitons. We decided it was time to comb the area of the Pitons, the Petit Piton and Piton LaCombe. This is where we witnessed a sight to behold. Several flocks of St. Lucia Amazons were feeding on fruits of the trees. Colors of blue, red, purple and green were evident.

Our guide told us that these birds nested in high hollow portions of trees, generally the acacia and licorice trees. They lay two eggs almost always and nest only once per year. Even though the parrots are protected, baby parrots are still stolen from the nesting holes. The babies are saved, however, as pets and perhaps as breeding stock. The sad state concerns those many St. Lucian Amazons that are shot to death for no apparent reason. Although there are a few hundred of these parrots on the island now, unless the authorities do something for their protection, this species will become extinct. Our visit and study of this Amazon was most educational. A visit to the natural environment of any parrot is worth a million words.

Further study of birdskins at Peabody Museum, Yale University revealed the true beauty of these birds. Their general plumage is green; the front and crown are blue fading to violet. Nape feathers are green to greenish blue with black tipping. The throat area is red in color, which is also dispersed throughout the abdominal area, fading to a reddish brown. Vent area and under the tail feathers are pale green. The upper tail coverts are yellowish green. Primary wing feathers are a blue-violet color; secondaries and some primaries have red feathers with green base and blue-violet to black tips. The bill is a grayish black with legs a light gray.

Further discussion on the over-all appearance of the breast and abdomen is worthwhile. The throat area appears bright red, fading to greenish feathering of the chest area with maroon splotches. The lower abdomen appears mainly maroon with flecks of occasional green. A superbly colored bird is this endangered species.

A few select pairs of St. Lucia Amazons are being imported into the United States under permit by United States Department of the Interior and United States Department of the Agriculture for breeding purposes. They are extremely rare in the States as well as continental Europe and Great Britain.

A record of breeding occurred in Bermuda in 1968. A young British couple have owned a pair of St. Lucia Amazons since 1965. The birds nested in a log set up in a flight laid out as a jungle. The flight was eight feet high, six feet long and seven feet wide. Two eggs were laid; twenty-eight days later the first chick hatched. The second egg hatched two days later; it had been laid two days later than the first. Both chicks were raised to adulthood and retained.

Apparently there are very few St. Lucia Amazons in the United States; some endangered species are prevalent in captivity, but not this one.

VINACEOUS AMAZON
Amazona vinacea

Aptly named for its color, the vinaceous Amazon is attractive, strikingly colorful and of excellent temperament. For an endangered species, there are quite a few vinaceous Amazons in the possession of aviculturists, zoos and private pet owners.

Perhaps the most beautiful pair of vinaceous Amazons I

have seen are exhibited on public display at the San Diego Zoo. These are large Amazons in excellent condition. In the mid 1970's, just before the bird was placed on the endangered species list, I was offered one pair of vinaceous Amazons for a mere three hundred dollars. For some reason I hesitated (as I often do); I regret it today.

In my studies of birdskins, at both Peabody Museum at Yale University and at the Los Angeles Museum of Natural History, I was mystified at the lustrous and vinaceous colors of this Amazon. The chin feathers are pink extending to a pinkish, purplish red throat and upper and lower breast. Hocks and lower abdomen are light green. The front is green, as are the crown and upper nape; however, the lower nape is bluish gray extending down the back.

This bluish gray extends around the side of the head to the throat. Occasional feathers are bluish gray tipped with rosy purple; others have rosy purple centers.

Wings are generally dark green, with primaries being green ending with blue tips. Secondaries have a red speculum on the first three feathers; blue and green complete the colors. The lateral tail feathers are basally red with dark green central areas ending in yellowish green. Concerning the bill, the base of the upper and lower mandibles are unique in being coral red. The extremely long feathers of the nape are noteworthy in that they can be held erect. Depending on the mood of the Amazon, the erected feathers are utilized. This could be to show irritation or gratitude. One vinaceous Amazon owned by a friend in Michigan spends fifty per cent of his time with his erected feathers standing high. The bird is very docile and loves to cackle to its owner at the same time. His favorite haunt is on his owner's desk in the library of the home. He will pick up a paper clip, erect his feathers and drop the clip in his owner's lap. This vinaceous Amazon, named Jimmy, loves to spend time in the kitchen. He has learned to turn on their osterizer (if it is plugged in); when it starts, his erectile

Amazona ochrocephala. With the most widespread range of any amazon, ten subspecific forms have been separated.

feathers go up and he squawks with loud, sharp and active caws, not unlike a crow. His exuberance lends much to this family in enjoyment and excitement.

GREEN-CHEEKED AMAZON, MEXICAN REDHEAD
Amazona viridigenalis

This Amazon is confused much too frequently with Finsch's Amazon as well as with the Lilacine and Salvin's Amazons. Hopefully this discussion will help all owners to differentiate among these birds.

The green-cheeked Amazon has a brighter green cheek area as well as a red front and crown. The red continues to almost the nape area of the bird. Note that the Lilacine, Salvin's and Finsch's Amazons have only red fronts; their crowns are not red in color.

The green-cheeked, also called Mexican redhead, has a general body plumage of green; each feather is edged in a dusky black. This bird has a blue band that goes from the base of the eyes to the nape of the neck. The primary coverts are green; the primaries are blue, turning green at the base. There is red at the base of the first five secondaries; others are blue, becoming green at the tips. The tail is green tipped with yellowish green. This species is found in northern Mexico, south to the state of Vera Cruz. Natives capture young from nesting holes, generally from cypress or acacia trees. Many of these young birds are hand-fed and tamed before they are sold for exportation to the states. The normal egg clutch in these hollow trees consistently has been two eggs. Thousands upon thousands of Mexican redheads have been imported into the United States. Some are exceedingly beautiful, and some become fair talkers.

240

In judging parrots at many bird shows I have seen strong classes of the Mexican redhead with much quality. Evidently there are many redheads from which to select a good show bird. Only the orange-cheek Amazon gives strong competition in numbers to the green-cheeked Amazon.

Green-cheeks have been known to hybridize with double yellow-heads. I have seen several of these hybrids; they appear attractive, but the yellow seems dominant about the head, and it is a lighter, paler yellow. The hybrids seem to come from the Guadalajara area of Mexico.

As a talker, *A. viridigenalis* is fairly good, but individual birds vary greatly in the quality of their mimicry. Much will also depend on the patience of the owner. One avid green-cheek owner has a superb bird that is a constant companion of an orange-wing Amazon. The owner has sold the green-cheek twice only to have it returned for lack of eating. This bird refuses to eat without the presence of the orange-wing. We understand that now both birds are for sale—but only together, with a guarantee that they always remain companions.

PUERTO RICAN AMAZON
Amazona vittata

As we stress throughout these pages, many of the precious Amazons are threatened and some are extremely close to extinction. Here is one Amazon that is dreadfully close to extinction. Only serious breeding and good hope and faith will preserve *Amazona vittata*, the Puerto Rican Amazon.

Having lived in Puerto Rico for close to two years, I spent many hours combing the mountain and rain forest of El Yunque looming in the proximity of Luquillo Forest. There is almost a constant cloud cover over El Yunque.

During this period in the early 1970's I saw only one Puerto Rican parrot.

It is a known fact that a certain few *Amazona vittata* individuals were taken to the Patuxent Wildlife Research Center in Maryland for attempts to successfully breed them and develop a captive population. Hopefully this plan might be helpful in preventing extinction. In 1965 there were approximately 100 Puerto Rican Amazons seen in the Luquillo Forest in eastern Puerto Rico. By 1972 there were no more than 15 to 20 seen.

There are many reasons why the Puerto Rican Amazon has become a dwindling species. The black rat and the mongoose, both mammals that were imported into Puerto Rico, perhaps have done more harm to the Puerto Rican Amazon than any other adverse factor.

Since the Puerto Rican Amazon nests in hollow trees, its most common competition for these hollows has been an aggressive bird called the pearly-eyed thrasher. In many cases the thrasher has actually pushed the Amazon out of its nesting sites.

It is certainly a fact that no Puerto Rican Amazons are owned by breeders and aviculturists. The only individuals in existence—other than a handful of birds in Luquillo Forest—do exist in Maryland. Perhaps those of us sighting a Puerto Rican Amazon may well recall the ending of an era. Let us hope not.

As in other Caribbean Amazons, the Puerto Rican has dark green feathers of the nape and back, each edged in black. The feathers of the throat, breast and abdomen appear lighter green. Occasionally tinges of black and red are seen as a scalloping effect on the breast feathers. Primary wing feathers and coverts are blue, while the secondary feathers are blue edged with green. Tail feathers are green to greenish yellow; bases of feathers have some red color. The forehead is red which extends only briefly to the lores. The eye ring is present and is white in color. The crown feathers are dark green, scalloped with black. The bill is yellow and legs are yellow.

I have not seen a Puerto Rican Amazon nest, but in talking to natives of Humacao, Luquillo and Rio Piedras in Puerto Rico I was told that there are generally always two eggs laid. For some unknown reason, very seldom would more than one chick emerge from the nest. Certainly there were exceptions; I was told that in some cases four chicks emerged.

One ardent admirer of the Puerto Rican Amazon stated that when he was a boy he enjoyed viewing the nesting behavior of one particular pair of birds. They would start nesting in a hollow which was fairly high in a large acacia tree. This nesting always occurred in February of each year. He would watch the antics of the male and female to a great degree. The female did all of the incubating; the male would return to the nesting hole several times per day and regurgitate to the female, thereby feeding her well. However, once per day at about 4 p.m. the female would leave the nest for about ten minutes. It was perhaps to secure water. At this time our friend climbed the acacia to view the nest. Each year there were two eggs. By the first of May the baby or babies would be out of the nest mingling with the adults. One year there would be two babies, the next year one baby. This repetitive affair occurred for another fourteen years, to the best of this old Puerto Rican's memory. Only once did three fledglings emerge from that nesting cavity. It is interesting to note that the same pair of Puerto Rican Amazons returned to the same acacia tree for nesting purposes at least fourteen years in a row. How wonderful! If only it could be accomplished in the Luquillo Forest today.

There is now some headway being made in the Puerto Rican mountains in breeding some of the native parrots. U.S. Dept. of the Interior personnel are placing nest boxes up in various areas that are not being bothered by the pearly-eyed thrasher; this dedicated service is creating a gradual increase of the magnificent Puerto Rican Amazon. By the spring of 1979, the count was close to thirty specimens.

A subspecies of *Amazona vittata* which is now extinct was originally found on the island of Culebra, northeast of the main island of Puerto Rico and almost directly north of the island of Vieques. This subspecies, *Amazona vittata gracilipes,* was called the Culebra Amazon. It was considerably smaller than the Puerto Rican Amazon. Unfortunately, all the parrots native to the island of Culebra are extinct. There are a few feral parrots on the island today, but their numbers are extremely small.

YELLOW-LORED AMAZON
Amazona xantholora

This Amazon, frequently found in the wilds of Mexico and Belize, is seldom imported and seldom seen in pet shops and aviaries in the United States. It amazes me to note the rarity in captivity of such a beautiful little Amazon.

Some authors and taxonomists place the yellow-lored Amazon in the same species as the white-fronted Amazons. However, they are different enough to warrant separation.

The front and forecrown are white, the lores are a bright yellow and the crown and hindcrown are blue. The nape of the neck and back feathers are dark green, with heavy black edging. This black edging is much more evident in the yellow-lored than in the white-fronted Amazons. The area around the eyes is bright red. The upper cheek areas are bright red. Ear coverts are black.

Primary coverts of the wing are red, more so in the male. Primary feathers of the wing are black, green and blue. Secondaries are mainly dark blue. The short and square tail is green, with yellowish green tips; lateral tail feathers have a red base extending to a yellowish green.

Young birds are rather ugly in that they lack the white front and most of the yellow of the lores, and the dark bluish black of the front and crown makes for a rather shabby-looking young bird. This could well be the reason so few are imported. They have not sold well on the few occasions they've been presented at pet shops.

The yellow-lored Amazon is easily confused with *Amazona albifrons* by many persons; perhaps this is the reasoning used by those who desire it to be considered as a subspecies of *A. albifrons*.

At least three aviculturists with whom I confer are owners of one or more yellow-lored Amazons. In each case it is remarkable that not one bird has even the slightest sign of a vocabulary. It would appear that this species has less initiative when it comes to mocking the human tongue. Others have made it known that certain individual yellow-lored Amazons do say a few words.

Perhaps aviculturists should attempt to breed this species in captivity. To the best of my knowledge, the yellow-lored has not been successfully hatched and reared in the United States.

YELLOW-BELLIED AMAZON
Amazona xanthops

My studies of several parrot skins at Peabody Museum, Yale University and the Los Angeles County Museum of Natural History became more intriguing when I thoroughly reviewed *Amazona xanthops*.

Firstly, this is a much smaller Amazon than the yellow-headed Amazons. Once an avid aviculturist sees the two

Amazons together, there is no problem in differentiating the two.

The head and neck of the yellow-bellied Amazon are yellow; the nape has green feathers edged with black. Ear coverts are yellow, while the breast feathers are green with a variable suffusion of yellow on each feather. As birds get older, the yellow suffusion becomes greater, even to a point of turning yellow-orange. Juveniles have very little yellow suffusion on the upper breast feathers. The abdomen of older birds becomes deep yellow to bright orange. It is a fascinating and beautiful bird.

Thighs are green. The tail feathers and tail coverts are yellowish green. Primary and secondary wing feathers are green with greenish yellow lacing or edging. The undersides of the flight feathers are a bluish green. The bill is light yellow to horn color.

Since this Amazon is found only in Brazil, it is doubtful that many imports will be seen, because Brazil is preventing the export of parrots and other birds at this time. There is no record of any *Amazona xanthops* imported into the United States during the past four years.

Noteworthy to mention, however, is the elderly couple that came through Nogales, Arizona with two pet birds on the way to New Hampshire. These two birds were legally imported, but the owners have no idea of the rarity of their birds, nor are they interested in knowing. They are merely interested in the pet aspect of the Amazons. They claim that they have two yellow-heads and they love them for the pets they are. They are not for sale, loan, breeding or public view. As a matter of fact, I was treated rudely as an intruder for just trying to see them. I was shown the birds; they were small, dainty ten-inch Amazons that were distinctly *Amazona xanthops*. It was well worth the rudeness I received. I was told that any person interested in breeding need not visit their premises. Their birds were pets and pets they would remain.

Yellow-naped Amazon, *Amazona ochrocephala auropalliata*. Photo by W. De Grahl.

Unfortunately, these were the only two *A. xanthops* in living flesh that I have ever seen. I don't want to deprive anyone from wanting pets—but, oh, if only the owners could be educated to the necessity of breeding the rare birds!

HAWKHEADED PARROT
Deroptyus accipitrinus

Most taxonomists and aviculturists will perhaps strongly disagree with my classification of the hawkheaded parrot, which I classify as a true Amazon, even though the bird is usually placed in the genus *Deroptyus,* which contains only one species, *D. accipitrinus.* My main classification characteristic involves the manner in which the hawkhead raises the hackle feathers of the nape. Several *Amazona* species have this ability. I have witnessed several of my collections of Amazons raising their hackle or nape feathers when excited. This, of course, is a typical trait of the hawkhead.

This is a most attractive bird. The colors are as symmetrical as any I have seen. The front and forecrown are creamy white; the hindcrown has feathers that are yellow, with brown edgings surrounding the entire feather. This blends into red feathers with outer blue scalloping that extends down the nape. Cheeks and lores have the yellow feathers which are surrounded entirely by brown. The feathers of the breast and abdomen are rich red with heavy blue edging. The thighs and flanks are green. Primary wing feathers are brownish black; wing coverts are green. Secondaries are green tipped with black. The tail is green tipped with blue. At the base of the tail is a maroon-colored area.

The hawkhead has been successfully bred in captivity in

the United States. An interesting pair of hawkheads hatched in this country were shipped to two homes in New England; one went to New Hampshire, the other to Connecticut. The hawkhead that went to New Hampshire was thought to be a male; it was a splendid hand-tamed pet that shared the home with about a dozen other fine parrots and became a chronic feather-picker. I was offered this male for five hundred dollars, an excellent price if he were not a feather picker. I didn't buy the bird, though, because I have three feather-pickers now, two macaws and a lorikeet. This hawkhead still lives in New Hampshire.

The female hawkhead turned out to be one of the most famous in the United States as both hawkhead and a parrot of quality. Three times she won Best Hookbill at the National Bird Show and at least once Best of All at the National. She was a beautiful show bird and always in immaculate condition. Her owner, Nancy Reed of Windsor, Connecticut, can well be proud. I can consider myself fortunate to have had this hawkhead presented before me as a judge.

In my travels to Surinam, in particular a safari through the jungle, my associates and I were thrilled to see a flock of six hawkheads flying to a palm tree where they stopped to watch our progress. They soon flew off in beautiful splendor. We attempted to look for nesting sites until I stepped on a large log—that moved. It turned out to be a giant anaconda. Needless to say, my search ended abruptly. That day I appreciated leaving the jungle.

Like most other Amazons, the hawkhead can readily be handled to become an excellent pet and companion. There are few Amazons that cannot be handled as long as you can prove to them that you are firm but gentle. Of the many hawkheads I have seen, literally all of them have been tame and fine to handle. All love to display with splendor in raising the hackle to extremes.

Index

Page numbers printed in **bold** refer to photographs or line illustrations.

252